# Happy and Glorious:
# The Constitution in Transition

# Studies in Law and Politics

Published by Open University Press in association with the
Centre for Criminological and Socio-Legal Studies

All enquiries regarding contributions and other editorial matters to:

Professor Norman Lewis, (General Editor)
Studies in Law and Politics, Unit for the Study of Law in Society
Faculty of Law, University of Sheffield
432 Crookesmoor Road
SHEFFIELD S10 1BL

Tel: (0742) 768555 (Ext. 6770)
Fax: (0742) 721319

# Happy and Glorious:
# The Constitution in Transition

*Edited by*

Norman Lewis, Cosmo Graham and Deryck Beyleveld

*With contributions from*

Lord Cockfield, Sir Douglas Wass, David Falcon,
Maurice Frankel and Bernard Crick

Open University Press
Milton Keynes - Philadelphia

Open University Press
Celtic Court
22 Ballmoor
Buckingham MK18 1XW

and
1900 Frost Road, Suite 101
Bristol, PA 19007, USA

First Published 1990

*British Library Cataloguing-in-Publication Data*
Happy and Glorious: the constitution in transition
(Studies in Law and Politics)
I. Great Britain. Constitutional Law
I. Lewis, Norman. II. Graham, Cosmo III. Beyleveld, Deryck
IV. Cockfield, Francis Arthur V. Series 344.102
ISBN 0-335-09487-2

*Library of Congress Cataloging-in-Publication Data*
Happy and Glorious : the constitution in transition / edited by Norman
Lewis, Cosmo Graham, and Deryck Beyleveld : with contributions
from Lord Cockfield ... [et al.].
p. cm. -- (Studies in law and politics)
Includes index.
ISBN 0-335-09487-2 (pbk).
1. Great Britain--Constitutional law. I. Lewis, Norman, 1940-. II.
Graham, Cosmo. III. Beyleveld, Deryck. IV. Cockfield, Lord. V.
Series.
KD 3989.H36 1990
342.73'02--dc20
[347-3022]
                                                              90-46748
                                                                   CIP
Printed in Great Britain by J.W. Arrowsmith Limited, Bristol.

# Contents

# Contributors

**Norman Lewis** is Professor of Public Law in the Unit for the Study of Law in Society, Faculty of Law, University of Sheffield. He is the joint author (with Ian Harden) of *The Noble Lie* and (with Ian Harden and Patrick Birkinshaw) of *Government by Moonlight*. He is currently doing research on both inner city initiatives and complaints procedures.

**Lord Cockfield,** Minister of State, Treasury, 1979-1982; Secretary of State for Trade, 1982-1983; Chancellor of the Duchy of Lancaster, 1983-1984; Vice President, Commission of the European Communities, 1985-1989.

**Sir Douglas Wass,** Chairman, Nomura International plc., and former joint head of U.K. Civil Service.

**David Falcon**, Director General of the Institute of Public Administration, formerly an Education Officer with Humberside County Council and the Inner London Education Authority.

**Maurice Frankel**, Director of the Campaign for Freedom of Information.

**Bernard Crick**, *Emeritus* Professor of Politics, Birkbeck College London and Honorary Fellow of the University of Edinburgh; author of *In Defence of Politics* and *George Orwell: A life*.

# Preface to the series

Norman Lewis

This is the first publication in what is to be a monograph series entitled *Studies in Law and Politics*. It is intended that three or four titles a year will be produced. Details of the Editorial Committee and the Editorial Advisory Committee can be found on p. ii.

As the series title suggests, we shall normally be publishing pieces which operate at the interface of law and politics, though the occasional monograph may be a pure piece of political science. The gap which the series is hoping to fill relates to sustained pieces of work which have a strong policy flavour. We shall, in general, be looking for work which is to some extent based upon empirical research, though naturally it will need to be grounded in some coherent theoretical tradition.

The established journals are usually unable to give space to publications of the length which the series will encourage; i.e. fifteen to twenty thousand words. Furthermore, publication deadlines are such that it is difficult to publish work which attempts to make a contribution to contemporary policy debates while the issues are still live. A primary aim of the series will be to stimulate policy debate at a time when it may still be possible to influence outcomes and before attitudes harden without the benefit of all the available information upon which decisions should be taken. British political life is notoriously unpluralistic and enjoys few of the checks and balances which characterise many of the constitutional orders of the major democracies. Think-tanks, of course, exist, but they are normally sheltered from contaminating external influences and it is fair to say that policy advice upon which vital national decisions are taken is not subject to the rigorous testing and scrutiny that many might think appropriate. The series cannot alter that state of affairs, but in its own small way intends to extend the information base upon which policy debate can take place.

Furthermore, by encouraging contributions which take on board serious, well-researched proposals for constitutional and political reform, we hope that we will contribute to making the British political system more open and responsive.

We also believe that the time is ripe to look outwards from Westminster and Whitehall towards Brussels, Strasbourg and Luxembourg. It is plain that the shape which our political and legal institutions will take in the years to come will be heavily influenced by events within the European Community. We shall then be particularly keen to attract titles which alert us to policy debates on the European stage.

# Introduction

Norman Lewis

It is perhaps ironic that the first title in the series should be untypical of what is to follow. However, it seemed to us desirable to launch the series in a celebratory fashion by holding a one-day conference. This we duly did on 26 January of this year. Having taken that step it seemed right and natural that we should publish the conference papers and a report of the proceedings in our first issue.

Although, therefore, this launch edition is not a sustained monograph, we believe that readers will find it rich and informative. Those who attended the conference clearly enjoyed it hugely and benefited from it considerably. I am sure our readership will share those experiences from a distance.

We were extremely fortunate to attract such a dazzling array of participants, not merely in terms of the main speakers but also on account of the distinction of those who chaired the sessions. Even so, I know that none of our distinguished guests will dissent from the view that Lord Cockfield, upon whom the University was delighted to confer the degree of LL.D., *honoris causa*, was very much the keynote speaker.

The theme and the title of the conference were chosen to contrast the rather cosy and self-satisfied series of assumptions that so often characterise public utterances about our constitutional arrangements and our system of politics, with the realities of a changing world which include UK membership of the European Community. The seventeenth century constitution, which was practically frozen in institutional terms in the nineteenth century, compares oddly with the systems of governance adopted by most of the Western democracies. It is, of course, true that in 1689 we did enjoy a very advanced form of political democracy in comparison with our neighbours, even if the overwhelming majority of our forebears were disenfranchised. It is also the case that we were one of the earliest nations to proclaim a Bill of Rights. However, only the most stubborn and illiterate apologist would now regard Britain as in the forefront either of democratic politics or of the promotion of the rule of law.

As so often is the case over a lengthy history, our national strengths are the reverse side of our national weaknesses. No-one should understate the enormous importance and value of the stability of our political and social life and of the strength born out of continuity. Yet that very stability has tended to petrification. There is a marked reluctance to examine our collective life anew, to start from first principles, systematically to engage in a wide-ranging examination of the way we operate. This is as true of our governing institutions as it is of our industrial and financial affairs. Everywhere is pragmatism and nowhere seemingly is rational re-appraisal.

However, the signs of change are all around us. Most notably that change can be detected in the noises coming from Brussels. Nothing, in European terms, will ever be the same again. The events of the seventeenth century will not be repeated and the history of the twenty-first century awaits us. Whatever lies out there it is certain that a European destiny awaits us. In consequence we shall have to learn new ways. Of course Britain has much to offer its European partners; but in many respects our institutional habits are out of tune with the rest of the Continent. This is most notably apparent in our legal system, and particularly in our system of *public* law which regulates the relationships between government and the governed. If non-discrimination across frontiers is to be practised then it is almost certain that we shall have to formalise, in legal terms, a number of new approaches to the business of government. Old accords, informality and networked arrangements, will be less acceptable than they have been in the past. It will be surprising if our system of public law does not have to make major concessions to the civil law systems in the near and middle future.

Suddenly regionalisation is also back on the agenda, partly again fired by the development of the European Community, but also on account of the mounting dissatisfaction of the Scots with their perceived lot. Some of the monographs planned in the near future address this theme in some surprising settings. Again it is unlikely that our legal and political understandings can remain undisturbed in the face of such developments.

It is, naturally, possible that many of our audience on 26 January were self-selecting and reformist by inclination; but much of the discussion seemed to assume that change was in the air and that our law and politics needed re-alignment. One of the exciting features of our new series is bound to be to see whether the contributions of scholars writing in this broad field underline that perception of a changing polity.

## The Contributions

Lord Cockfield's views about the European Community have become widely publicised in recent years and so perhaps little of what he says about the balance of power between Brussels and Westminster should surprise our readers, especially given his active role in promoting the goal of European Monetary Union and his part in producing the Single European Act. Even so, the forcefulness of his remarks, and the passion with which he invites us to grasp the fact of the new European order, may surprise many.

In Lord Cockfield's view our membership of the Community was a constitutional revolution of a very real kind. In drawing parallels with the Statute of Westminster 1931 he reminds us that accession to the Treaties and to the Community were no mere legislative phenomena, but an acceptance of the fact that the world had changed and had changed us with it. The British people have been slow to accept change; perhaps reluctant to accept it, and this may in no small measure help to account for the success of successive generations of politicians and constitutionalists in clinging to old beliefs and accords, and in particular to old institutional frameworks, when the world had irremediably altered. All the other contributors to this volume argue the case for constitutional change in their different ways and in doing so are in tune with the voices of many other contemporary students of our politics and legal order. Until recently, however, there has been more agreement about the shortcomings of our system than about the likelihood of their early remedy. Yet suddenly the European future seems incompatible with British institutional habits in so many ways. This is very much at the heart of Lord Cockfield's advice. There is no going back; we can only opt out and let the changes occur without any contribution from us. Temporising and obstructing are not really options; only creative engineering makes any sense. This means that there is enormous scope for devising open and accountable mechanisms for the instruments of policy formation and delivery. The message is that those committed to constitutional and administrative reform should not be faint-hearted. Instead they should commit themselves to hard work and clear thinking, so that when proposals emerge for the new Europe there will be enough sophisticated policy thinking available to enable us to deliver on the democratic beliefs embedded in the European ideal.

In the meantime, if Britain is to object to bureaucratic brutality or closeted decision-making in Brussels then it should not be vulnerable to accusations that Westminster is an insensitive and compliant handmaiden of Whitehall and other interests. This concern lies behind David Falcon's proposals for a National Office of Policy Analysis which would assist with pre-legislative debates about major policy initiatives. Coming from the new Director-General of the Royal Institute for Public Administration, it may be expected that such proposals would carry considerable weight. Whatever reservations individuals might entertain, there is no doubt that such a development would greatly strengthen democratic debate at Westminster and bring us much further into line with both Washington DC and Paris. Aligning oneself with French constitutional rationalism might augur well for the debates yet unborn about the ultimate constitutional shape of the new Europe.

Bernard Crick makes a number of challenging remarks in a characteristically robust style. He sees the Act of Union not as a re-affirmation of Westminster's omnicompetence, but as a device directed towards crisis management. He argues that a 'balanced' constitutional relationship was implicit both in the events of the time and the cultural expectations of the Scots, a culture understood by the old 'Tories' of the times. In this, the events surrounding the passage of the Act shared much with the English constitutional settlement of 1688-9. An omnicompetent Parliament (especially one dominated by the executive) was not contemplated by the overwhelming body of those most active in the events of the period. The practice of discourse and a series of self-denying ordinances accompanied the politics of the time and the constitutional thinking of the informed nation. Time it was, and the emergence of the party system, which kidnapped the settlement and produced an undifferentiated substitution of the divine right of the (largely English) executive for the Divine Right of Kings.

Crick seems to be arguing that the people are in the mood to reclaim their heritage, with the Scots leading the way. He is clear in his own mind that indivisible means indivisible and that divisible may as well be by six or eight as by two. We shall see.

Maurice Frankel's piece on Freedom of Information (FOI) is written in a racy and amusing style which is guaranteed to entertain our readers. Maurice's credentials in the FOI field are second to none and many have long been convinced by the power and the lucidity of his arguments. However, what will strike most people is the simple, elegant and witty fashion in which he destroys the traditionalist's claim about the sovereignty of Parliament as a debating and questing chamber. In a few pages he demolishes the unsustainable claims of the more staid constitutional textbooks with a force which many of us have taken a generation to seek to produce. It will be required reading for my students in future. I suspect I shall not be alone.

I have pleasure in introducing the proceedings of the 'Happy and Glorious' Conference of 26 January 1990 which consist of the four conference papers and Sir Douglas Wass's measured response to Lord Cockfield's address.

# The Constitution in Transition: The Balance of Power: Brussels and Westminster

Lord Cockfield

May I start by congratulating the University of Sheffield and particularly Professor Norman Lewis on the launch of this new series which deals essentially with the way the British constitution is developing. It comes at a time when these issues have become matters of serious, if not at times acrimonious, debate in this country, particularly in regard to our own relations with the European Community. That debate has at times been obfuscated by the fact that we in this country, in contrast with our Community partners, do not have a written constitution: by the fact that we enjoy a differing system of law: and by the fact that the Community, following continental precedent, does have its own 'written constitution' in the form of its founding treaties as amended, *inter alia*, by the Single European Act. This is one of the principle reasons why we in this country so often fail to understand both the inherent nature or spirit of the Community and the nature and manner of its development. Too often ministers treat the treaties and Community legislation in much the same way as a tax avoidance lawyer approaches a taxing statute; namely, how does one avoid the impact of the statute rather than how does one give effect to its manifest intention? Inevitably, therefore, a study of the British constitution must widen out into a study of the impact of external events and particularly our membership of the European Community on our constitutional arrangements. And that is why I (a European as well as a British citizen) have been asked to give this opening address.

## The Balance of Power

In the 19th century the foreign policy of this country was directed to preserving the balance of power in Europe, in some respects a cynical policy but one which in earlier times had considerable advantages. The policy was continued into the 20th century long after its real justification had disappeared, and with appalling consequences. We now see it re-emerging again in our response to the epoch-making changes in eastern Europe. But this is a different century from the last century and the second half of this century is very different from the first half. The first half was a period of bitter conflict: the second half was devoted to the construction of a new Europe based upon co-operation not conflict: a new Europe which was designed to preserve the peace not foster war. The philosophy which underlay this change in approach was that it was economic rivalry, a struggle to secure resources, which sowed the seeds of war. It followed therefore that the way to avoid war and preserve peace was to substitute economic co-operation for economic rivalry, and so the European Community was born.

Inevitably a change of policy and philosophy of such historical dimensions is bound to create conflicts. The most important of these conflicts centres on the division of power between the Community at the centre and the governments of the individual member states. So we see emerging the quest for a new 'balance of power' between the Community and the member states; in our own case between Brussels and Westminster. Hence the title of this address.

## British Accession to the European Community

We joined the European Community in 1973. There are many people in this country who talk and act as though that was the first dawn, the moment of creation: that we had a *tabula rasa* on which we could write anything that took our fancy. That view is entirely mistaken. The Community came into being in the immediate aftermath of the second of the great wars which devastated Europe in the first half of this century: not even in 1957, as so many people think, but in 1952 when the Treaty of Paris set up the first of the 'communities' - the Coal and Steel Community. Coal and steel were regarded as the sinews of war: hence their choice as the first venture into co-operation instead of conflict. That they were the first step along a new road comes out very clearly in the preamble to this Treaty which looked ahead to the establishment of an economic community. The actual words of the Treaty - which are very significant for the future, both in this and a wider context - were as follows:

> Resolved to substitute for age-old rivalries the
> merging of their essential interests:  to create, by
> establishing an economic community, the basis for a
> broader and deeper community among peoples long
> divided by bloody conflicts:  and to lay the
> foundations for institutions which will give direction
> to a destiny henceforth shared ...

In due course the Treaty of Paris was followed in 1957 by the Treaty of
Rome which established the economic community envisaged by the
Treaty of Paris and a second treaty which established the Atomic
Energy Community.

So that when we joined the Community in 1973 it was already 21
years old.  It had already reached maturity.  It had developed a whole
range of policies extending far beyond freedom of trade and we were
obliged, under the terms of the Treaty of Accession, to accept the
policies the Community had developed.  It is our failure to understand
this, or the failure of the present generation of politicians to understand
this, which lies at the root of so many of the difficulties which have arisen
between ourselves and our fellow members of the Community.

## European Union

From the very beginning the objective was 'European Union', certainly
in the economic field and, in the view of many people, the political field
as well.  The very first recital of the Treaty of Rome, which established
the European Community essentially as we now know it today, reads:
'Determined to lay the foundations of an ever closer union among the
peoples of Europe'.  The 'solemn declaration on European union',
subscribed to at Stuttgart in June 1983 and signed by the heads of
government of all the member states and their foreign ministers,
including our present Prime Minister and the then Foreign Secretary
(Sir Geoffrey Howe),  carried the matter a significant step forward.
The Single European Act, negotiated at Luxembourg in December
1985,  now provides the keystone of the arch.

It is important to realise how extensive are the policies of the
community as set out in the Single Act.  They comprise -

- ° The internal market
- ° Economic and monetary union
- ° Social policy
- ° Economic and social cohesion
- ° Research and technological development
- ° The environment
- ° Political co-operation in the field of foreign policy.

In many instances the implementation of these policies will require further subordinate legislation. But it is a complete fallacy and entirely contrary to the Community ethos to argue, as some ministers in this country have done, that they are entitled to frustrate the policies laid down in the Single Act by blocking or attempting to block the legislation required to give effect to those policies. It is an attitude which is completely unacceptable to our Community partners and I would have hoped unacceptable to most people in this country.

**National Sovereignty**

Central to the discussion of these matters, and particularly how they affect our own country and our own constitutional position, is the question of 'national sovereignty' and the impact upon 'national sovereignty' of developments in the Community. So much has been written and spoken recently about sovereignty, not least by myself, that it would be otiose, not to say tedious, to repeat all the arguments here. But some comment is essential.

In one of my early speeches (Cockfield 1986) in Brussels, I said this:

> 'National sovereignty' for the nineteenth century politician had a clear sense. Internally it was the ability of a country's government to make and implement decisions which it saw as being in its own national interest. Externally sovereignty consisted in defending one's own national interests against other countries: by force if needs be.

Sovereignty thus seen had therefore two aspects; an internal one and an external one. Internally the concept of national sovereignty had been rationalised by constitutional lawyers such as Maitland, Dicey and Austin who saw 'national sovereignty' as an expression of the absolute sovereignty of Parliament. When I first read law in the 1930s Dicey was still a formidable voice. But the world in which he lived and wrote was already passing away. In 1931 the Statute of Westminster finally transferred 'sovereignty' to the Dominions. This was not just a legislative act but one which recognised the change which had occurred in the real world. Anyone who would now suggest that the absolute sovereignty of the Westminster Parliament would extend to the repeal of the Statute of Westminster has long since departed from reality. That this is so is illustrated by the case of the 'patriation' of the Canadian constitution where the government and parliament at Westminster accepted that they must legislate in accordance with the wishes of the government and parliament at Ottawa. Perhaps just as significant as these developments, the European Communities Act of 1972 transferred a large, and increasing, measure of sovereignty to the European Community.

Externally the change was less formalised but even more fundamental. The bloody climax of the theory of national sovereignty was seen in the first of the great wars which devastated Europe in the first half of this century. *'Si monumentum requiris circumspece'*. The monument to the theory and even worse the practice of national sovereignty is to be seen in the millions upon millions of graves marching across the landscape of Europe. 'Lest we forget' we sing on Remembrance Day. But too many have forgotten.

Whether in war or in peace, the world has changed in a way which would make it unrecognisable to the nineteenth century constitutional theorists. The world of Rudyard Kipling has all but disappeared. No longer is it true that: 'East is east and west is west and never the twain shall meet'. The whole world has become interdependent and interlocking. The development of international agencies and bodies: the old League of Nations and the present United Nations; the GATT; Bretton Woods; the Convention on Human Rights with its own Court of Justice at Strasbourg, and, most important of all, the European Community; all of these represent a significant erosion of the concept of exclusive national sovereignty. Outside the institutional field, the development of international trade and even more so the development and massive power of the financial markets mean that in large measure national sovereignty over economic matters has drained away.

That 'east is east and west is west' is true only to the extent that Tokyo starts trading before London and London before New York. All these are joined together with an information network operating, not with the five miles an hour that the British rifleman achieved in Victorian times, but with the speed of light.

Against this background I would only say that to those of us whose political and legal experience has extended over many of the events I have described, it is a matter of great surprise to find the pure milk of the nineteenth century constitutional theory of national, and particularly parliamentary, sovereignty surfacing once again, as though nothing had happened in the last one hundred years. 'Victorian values', or at least some of them, may have virtue. But trying to wipe out one hundred years of history is not one of them. Until I went to Brussels and found myself in disagreement, if not conflict, with our own government here in Westminster on matters of this kind, I had always thought that Rip van Winkle was a fictional character.

One of the more absurd examples of inventing parliamentary sovereignty as an argument against European integration lies in the basis on which monetary union has been opposed by the present government. They claim that control of monetary policy is the very foundation stone of parliamentary sovereignty. The argument is both absurd and fallacious, as anyone with even a passing knowledge of British constitutional history would know. I set out the position in some detail in a speech I delivered in the House of Lords on 18 December 1989 (514 HL Debs, cols 13-16). Briefly, the position is that monetary policy came into the hands of the government only with the nationalisation of the Bank of England at the instance of Mr. Hugh Dalton, as he then was, in 1946. Even then it was not until 1973 with the final breakdown of the Bretton Woods system that government and the politicians secured complete control: and what a disaster it has been. The true foundation stone of parliamentary sovereignty in this country is the control of public expenditure and raising taxation to meet it. That was the issue which set light to the conflagration which became the civil war (*R v Hampden* (1637) 3 St.Tr. 825) and it was the victory of the parliamentary forces which set the seal on what we now call parliamentary sovereignty. Indeed I doubt whether John Hampden had even heard of monetary policy.

I appreciate that there are those in this country who are opposed even to our membership of the Community, and a great number, not least in our own government, who take a restricted view of what the Community is and whose vision is limited to 'free trade'. I propose, assuming that we here today do understand the true nature of the Community, that we are prepared to abide by the commitments we have entered into, and that we are prepared to take a full part in the development of European Union to which we committed ourselves both in the solemn declaration and in the Single European Act. This is, I would hope, a majority view in this country even if it is not fully shared by the government, or perhaps I should say not shared by the full government.

We have a further problem in this country, not shared by our fellow member states, and that is the way the Parliament at Westminster has kept the British members of the European Parliament at arm's length. Marginally matters have improved recently, but the fundamental divide still exists in a way that is quite untypical on the continent. It is customary in other countries for individuals to move back and forth in a way that the political system and political traditions in this country make impossible. Thus we see Giscard D'Estaing, former President of France, and still with ambitions for the future, becoming a member of the European Parliament. So too has Leo Tindemanns, for 17 years Foreign Minister of Belgium. Jacques Delors himself has been, successively, a member of the European Parliament, Finance Minister of France and President of the European Commission: and he could well return to government in France. Martin Bangemann, the German Vice-President, has a similar history. We would be better served in this country if we could boast a few members of our own Cabinet with that kind of experience.

So these arguments about 'sovereignty' are the last twitch of the dragon's tail. I have no doubt that you and others will continue to debate it. But for my part I think it more important to accept that fundamental change has occurred and that it will not be reversed. The days when we could block progress in the Community have gone. All we can do is to opt out, either on specific issues or generally. That is not a course I would want us to take and I assume that in the end it is not a course we would take. What we now need to do therefore is to consider what is the best and most productive way of managing the new situation.

**The Division of Powers - The Principle of Subsidiarity**

In recent years it has become fashionable to invoke the principle of subsidiarity. It is not a new concept and in many ways it is a development of the old argument about centralisation and decentralisation. Like so many 'general principles' it is much more attractive in dissertation than in practice. In practice it needs to be applied at two different levels. First, what major areas of policy need to be decided at the top level, at the Community level, or at the federal level if we move towards a federal Europe. Second, within the areas appropriate to the Community or federal level, how much should the top level actually do and how much should be delegated to the lower or state level? The issue exists at present but it becomes more acute as the powers of the Community extend and, *a fortiori,* if we move to a federal system.

Let me give a simple, and I hope uncontentious, example based on current experience. The creation of a true common market in which goods, services, people and capital move freely clearly requires a great deal of legislation at the top or Community level. Originally the course followed was to legislate in great detail at the Community level. However, progress was extremely slow. In 1985 the Commission, of which I was Vice-President, developed what was called 'the new approach'. Originally this concept was applied to the standards applicable to the manufacture of industrial goods but I extended the principle to other fields, particularly the financial services. Under the 'new approach' a basic framework specifying the 'essential requirements' is laid down at Community level, and writing the detailed standards is left to the standards-making bodies in the member states; the British Standards Institute in this country, the German Institute for Normalisation, the French Association for Normalisation and so on. Provided these standards comply with the framework Directive, then goods made to these standards are entitled as of law to freedom of circulation throughout the Community.

The 'new approach' has led to rapid progress being made; but it also illustrates a fundamental problem. Freedom of circulation is one thing; but this is no good if, for example, the infrastructure of other countries does not permit the goods actually to be used. A simple example is the electric plug. A British plug, while legally entitled to free circulation in other countries, simply cannot be used because the sockets on the continent are different from those in the UK. So one is still left with the practical need to manufacture to meet the requirements of the local market. The only way this problem can be solved is by the adoption of *European* standards so that goods can both legally and in practice be used in all member states. This in fact is what has now been done in the case of television equipment and mobile telephones. In short, the facts of the market-place compel the Community itself to legislate. So that, in an area in which the intention was to delegate to the member states in conformity with the principle of subsidiarity, the facts of life compel the Community as the top level of 'government' to take the powers back again. So the theory has to accommodate itself to the needs of the market-place. In a country such as our own, devoted to the principle of market forces, it is important to recognise that the market forces themselves often demand legislation in order to enable them to operate.

### The Division of Powers - Accommodating to the Change

There has been a great deal of criticism of the comment made by Jacques Delors, in a speech to the European Parliament, that in ten years' time 80 per cent of legislation on economic matters and possibly on social matters would be Community legislation. Whether the ten years is correct or the 80 per cent is right, I would not attempt to judge: but the general comment that increasingly legislation, certainly in the economic field, will be Community legislation must be right. This is illustrated very clearly in the example I have just given. It is simply no good getting indignant about this. All change is unpalatable to those adversely affected - in this instance of course the government and parliament at Westminster - but if the change is inevitable, then the right reaction is not opposition but 'How does one accommodate to it?'.

The next step, therefore, once we have decided what the likely division of power or competence between Westminster and Brussels is likely to be, is to ask ourselves how best we, in Westminster, can accommodate ourselves to this change. In the Community at large there are two different approaches. In Denmark, for example, the Folketing, through its market committee, keeps the government on a very short rein and insists on prior approval of everything ministers do. At the other extreme, in some countries, ministers are given a very wide discretion; their actions are regarded as within the competence of the government and it is the government's responsibility to justify *ex post* its actions to its own parliament. We have hitherto tended very much to fall into the latter category. The House of Commons, however, has now woken up to the implications of the Community for its own functioning powers, and I gave them some assistance in this direction in the evidence I gave to the Select Committee on European Legislation. It clearly feels it should now play a more active role.

What advice, help or indeed guidance, would we as constitutional lawyers or experts wish to offer them? There is a real area of conflict here because attempts to *control* what government does, as opposed to steps to *influence*, create two distinct and opposite risks. Thus it may greatly slow down the pace of European development - and remember that much of this development is in our own interest despite what is so often said in public. Conversely, obstructing progress or even simple dilatoriness may result in our being left behind or ignored. This risk is significantly increased by the greater use of majority voting and indeed by the greater tendency of the Community as a whole to move away from the concept of 'unanimity'. In short, accepting that we are no longer total masters in our own house - and, despite indignant protests in some quarters, have not been total masters in our own house for very many years - what should our approach be when it comes to suggesting to our government and our legislators what their approach should be?

### Misconceptions about a "Brussels Bureaucracy"
Before I leave this aspect of the division of powers between Brussels and Westminster, I must comment on the claims so often made in this country that we should be transferring power from a 'democratic' Westminster to an 'unelected Brussels bureaucracy'. The language used itself indicates that this is an appeal to prejudice and not an intellectual argument; but it needs to be dealt with. May I take, by

way of example, the leader which appeared in the Daily Telegraph on 8 December immediately before the Strasbourg Summit. Headed 'The Strasbourg Spirit' and discussing 'our attitude to Europe', it referred to 'Relinquishing power or sovereignty to a largely unrepresentative Brussels bureaucracy'. Furthermore, it described this as 'That main issue which troubles many people in this country'.

This is complete nonsense. The transfer of power to the Community is not a transfer to a Brussels bureaucracy. The last word on Community legislation rests with the Council of Ministers which consists of *ministers* - note ministers. It cannot consist even of national officials from the governments of the individual member states. If the Daily Telegraph regards those governments, and in this context particularly our own government, as 'unrepresentative' there may be something in it. Indeed it would have the support of Lord Hailsham, the former Lord Chancellor, who described the British government as an 'elective dictatorship'. He was talking of a previous government but the comment applies *a fortiori* to our present government. I doubt however whether this is what the Daily Telegraph had in mind.

If the comment was intended to refer specifically to monetary union, which it clearly did not, as it was couched in wide and general terms, then it is still inaccurate. The proposal in the Delors committee report was to set up a committee of central banks which by no stretch of the imagination could be described as 'Brussels bureaucrats'. Presumably the term 'unrepresentative' is intended to mean 'not democratically elected'. In fact, monetary policy is supremely the one area in which democratic control has been demonstrated to be an unqualified disaster. One only has to look at the fate of the pound sterling over the years compared with the Deutschmark, where monetary policy is determined by the Bundesbank, which under the terms of the federal constitution is independent of government. I remember the days, not so very many years ago, when the pound was worth *ten* deutschmark. Today it cannot even look *three* deutschmark in the face. If this is the kind of democratic control the Daily Telegraph wants, we are better off without it.

There is a case, not with monetary union but elsewhere, to strengthen the powers of the European Parliament. This is what Chancellor Kohl and many others want. But it is bitterly opposed by Mrs. Thatcher, whose contempt for the European Parliament is beyond belief.

## The Institutions of the Community

Linked to the question of the relationship between Westminster and Brussels is the question of the relationship of the institutions in the Community to one another.  The institutional structure of the Community is based upon Montesquieu's theory of the separation of powers;  that there should be an executive, a legislature and a judiciary independent of one another.  When I was a student I was taught that Montesquieu's theory was based on a misunderstanding of the British constitution.  Be that as it may, the American constitution is a prime example of the theory being translated into practice:  and so is the constitution of the European Community.  The Commission is the executive arm of the Community charged with the power of management, endowed with the right of initiative and established as 'the guardian of the treaties'.  Of course, its powers are infinitely less than the powers of the executive in the United States; but that reflects the very much more restricted powers of the Community, as compared with the powers of the federal government in the United States.  The legislative function is shared between the Council of Ministers and the European Parliament, while the judicial function is represented by the Court of Justice in Luxembourg.

Over the years the Council has encroached significantly on the powers of the Commission.  The Single Act, however, turned, or sought to turn, the tide, and increased both legal and *de facto* powers of the Commission.  The appointment of a very strong and determined President in Jacques Delors was also a powerful force operating in the same direction.  Unfortunately, the Council of Ministers has largely failed to implement the increased delegation of powers to the Commission as the Single Act intended.

At the same time, the European Parliament has extended, or sought to extend, its powers in two directions.  First, by greater participation in the legislative process.  Thus the Single Act introduced the 'co-operation procedure' for internal market matters. Although this fell far short of what the Parliament wanted, it has in fact proved a significant step forward both in terms of giving the Parliament an effective voice in the formation of legislation, and in enabling it to act as a 'revising chamber' in much the same way as does the House of Lords, thus improving the *quality* of legislation.  Second, it has sought, so far unsuccessfully, to exercise some direct control over the Commission by giving it a say in the appointment of the President, or indeed of other members, and by making the Commission answerable to the Parliament.  While great co-operation between the Commission and Parliament is highly desirable - and I myself did much to improve matters in the areas for which I was responsible - I have always felt that any legal control by the Parliament over the Commission was contrary to basic principle and would lead in due course to direct confrontation between Parliament and Council which the present system, with the Commission as honest broker in the middle, has done much to avoid.

The argument about the 'democratic deficit' in the Community largely centres around attempts to increase the powers of the European Parliament more generally. As I have already mentioned, Chancellor Kohl at the Strasbourg Summit strongly supported such moves. But it would be just as important to 'democratize' the Council of Ministers and insist that they should operate in public. I mention these matters because the balance of power between the institutions of the Community, and the efforts to increase the power of the Parliament in particular, are bound to have an effect on the balance of power between the member states and the Community: specifically in our own case between Brussels and Westminster.

## Conclusion

I have covered a wide range of issues in this address. My purpose has been to expose these issues to debate rather than to suggest answers, although in some instances you may feel that my personal views and reactions have peered cautiously above the parapet. In talking to an audience like this and on an occasion like this, the most important question is to decide what issues need to be addressed. Indeed, to those of us upon whom it falls the duty or the pleasure of delivering speeches or lectures, deciding what to talk about is much more difficult than deciding what to say once you have decided what to talk about. So with both confidence and relief I leave it to the University of Sheffield and the authors of the individual studies in the series launched today to give us their analysis, their perception, and their prescription for the future.

## Reference

Cockfield, Lord (1986) *Studia Diplomatica*, 39, 649-657.

# Comment

Sir Douglas Wass

It will come, I think, as no surprise to this audience to learn that I am in substantial sympathy with almost everything Lord Cockfield had to say; but there were one or two elements in his address where my thoughts ran in a slightly different direction and I would like to discuss them briefly and offer some reflections.

On the question of sovereignty which Lord Cockfield dealt with so trenchantly, it seems to me we have a peculiarly British, perhaps English, hang-up and we have to ask ourselves why this is so. In my view we have to look to our history to obtain our clues to this question why other countries, and certainly those who have revised their constitutions and put them down in writing, don't have that hang-up. When we talk about sovereignty, we mean national sovereignty, and the sovereignty that comes to mind is the sovereignty of Parliament. 'The sovereignty of Parliament' is the expression that springs to the lips of politicians and parliamentarians. Now the sovereignty of Parliament was born in the Glorious Revolution, the constitutional revolution in the seventeenth century, when sovereignty *de jure* was transferred from the Monarch, the King himself, to Parliament. We, in this country, have not progressed any further with the devolution of sovereignty. Sovereignty is still firmly lodged with Parliament. Contrast this with the United States, whose constitution firmly embeds sovereignty with the people, not with the Congress, not with the

President. That distinction between the sovereignty of Parliament and the sovereignty of the people lies at the very heart of so many of the political difficulties we have in this country today. They are not only difficulties in our relations with Europe, which are bedevilled by the thought of anything but the U.K. Parliament being sovereign. The European Parliament, for instance, or the Commission is complete anathema to us. The distinction I referred to affects also the whole question of central and local government relations in the United Kingdom, where local democracy is deemed to be no greater than Parliament in its wisdom will allow. By contrast in many other systems the ultimate authority, the ultimate legitimacy, lies with the people and it is for the people to decide by due process, for instance by referendum, where power shall reside. I think we need to ask ourselves where in a modern democracy should legitimacy lie? Does it lie with an institution like Parliament by virtue of history or does it in fact lie, where I believe it should lie, with the people and should there be constitutional mechanisms for the people to express their views?

Seeing Maurice Frankel in the audience, I am moved to make a small and I hope relevant diversion. I think our whole attitude to freedom of information derives from this historical issue of where sovereignty lies. The entrenched attitude of the establishment in this country is that government information belongs to the government and that if the government is to share it with anyone it is with Parliament as the sovereign body. The government sees itself as a Parliamentary institution - 'the King in Parliament' - and if it is going to cede power to anyone else, that 'anyone else' is only Parliament. In the United States, however, you find a universal acceptance that government information is public information because the public is the supreme authority. Public information belongs to the people, unless there is good cause why it should not. So you see this question of Parliamentary sovereignty has become a stumbling block to a great many reforms, among which those affecting Europe are only a part.

My second comment is about economic and monetary union. What Lord Cockfield had to say about the sovereignty of monetary policy was very revealing and indeed very apt. But I believe that the act of creating economic and monetary union in Europe will involve a real transfer of sovereignty. It is not a transfer that I oppose, but I think that we would do well to recognise that it throws up some very important issues of principle and issues of policy. It is not simply a question of putting together a federation of central banks or of tying sterling irrevocably and irreversibly to a new European currency like the ECU. If we are going to create a single currency area - and I believe we shall, for the forces pushing towards the creation of that are now very strong indeed and probably irresistible - then I think we have to take our thinking beyond the Delors Report. We have to face the implications this has for the way we run our affairs and for the way we ensure that there are not too many disparities in employment and income and welfare within the community. I find the debate within the Community on what the exchange rate mechanism of the European Monetary Union (EMU) should be and what EMU amounts to strangely deficient in that it has not addressed itself to the question of the disparities in income, employment and welfare that can arise from, and be intensified by, the creation of a single currency area. I know of no system in the world where there is a single currency area where there is no centralisation to some extent of fiscal policy and no strong system of resource allocation from wealthy areas to less wealthy areas. The important aspect of sovereignty which stems from the existence of a national currency lies in the ability of a sovereign government to change the exchange rate between its own currency and that of other currencies, and so ensure that economic activity in its domain is not depressed because of the imperfections of internal markets. Exchange rate adjustment is a policy instrument which pretty well every government of the twentieth century has had to employ at some stage even in a floating rate environment. If that instrument of sovereignty is taken away, as it will be taken away in European monetary union, then the individual national governments will have no greater power than do individual local authorities today within a nation state to affect the employment and income and aggregate welfare of their citizens. The Community, therefore, has to assume a new and important responsibility if it is to deal with this problem and not sweep it under the carpet, as so far it has. The Community has to take the power to make very substantial transfers of resources, analogous to those transferred under a regional policy, or it has to take very substantial items of public expenditure and very substantial powers of taxation from national governments, so as to ensure, to some extent at any rate, that the entitlement to public benefits within the Community is based on need and the obligation to finance them is based on ability to pay. Without some such centralisation of the power to tax and the power to spend there will be a gaping hole in economic and monetary union as it has been put forward.

Vice-Chancellor, ladies and gentlemen, I have chosen those two items for comment; they both spring to some extent from Lord Cockfield's address although they go somewhat beyond his ambit. I do not expect him to agree with the second of my points that I have made because I have been in dispute on it with his successor in Brussels. But I hope that he would agree that it is an important issue that needs public airing. Public opinion must address itself to the substantial transfer of sovereignty which will be required when economic and monetary union is achieved. Vice-Chancellor, I am sure that I speak on your behalf, and on behalf of everyone in this audience, in expressing our thanks to Lord Cockfield for his very stimulating, very interesting, and highly authoritative address.

# Public Administrators and Constitutional Reform

David Falcon

Risking comparison with John Banham's view of those lacking precision in their thinking, that 'generally speaking he was generally speaking', may I start by suggesting that the essence of the constitutional reform debate is about the checks and balances that need to exist between those who are elected to govern and those who are governed. Much of today's proceedings will focus on those two categories of people; whether the governed are citizens or subjects; whether their interests are best protected by overarching Bills of Rights or by more specific legislative action; what information should those who govern make available to the governed; what should the relationship be between the two Houses of Parliament and the government, and between governments at the European, United Kingdom and Scottish/Welsh/Regional level? I want to make my contribution from a different perspective; from the perspective of those who are employed to assist in the process of government: public administrators.

I have chosen the phrase public administrators rather than civil servants very deliberately to ensure that we do not forget those who work in local government, in the national health service and in other areas of the public service.

In this paper I am attempting to relate three strands. Firstly, a code of ethics that public administrators should observe for the public to have confidence in their stewardship of the public interest. Secondly, a comparison of the current situation in local government, the health service and the civil service and an attempt to demonstrate the way in which the secrecy of the policy formulation process potentially corrodes this code. Finally, I will make a proposal for a new form of pre-legislative policy analysis, which some may find implausible but which, I believe, will help us consider the relationship between the behaviour of individual public administrators and the constitutional framework within which they work.

Peter Hennessy, who is a Visiting Fellow at the RIPA amongst his other distinctions, delivered the 1989 First Division Association GCHQ Commemorative Lecture on 'The Ethic of the Profession' (Hennessy 1989). He identified the characteristics of a 'Genetic Code' for the senior ranks of the civil service which seem to me to be equally applicable to all parts of the public service:-

° Probity;
° Care for evidence;
° Respect for reason;
° Willingness to speak truth unto power;
° Capacity not just to live with the consequence of what is conceived to be a mistaken course, but to pursue it energetically;
° Awareness of other people's life chances;
° Equity and fairness;
° Constant and careful concern for the law;
° Constant concern for Parliament, its needs and procedures;
° Concern for democracy.

Hennessy is concerned that this genetic code of professional expectations should be transmitted from one generation of civil servants to the next. What conditions need to exist to assist this transmission?

Clearly a great deal has to do with selection, peer group conditioning and more overt forms of personal development and performance review, both formal and informal. These are all personal interactions between people who, hopefully, are committed to this genetic code. Attention has been given, particularly by civil service unions and local government professional associations, to the value of codes of conduct. Indeed one might expect the civil service itself to promote such a written code. As a result of a number of well publicised cases, the then Head of the Home Civil Service produced guidance for civil servants in 1985 (Armstrong 1985). In his note of guidance he states:

> The civil service as such has no constitutional personality or responsibility separate from the duly elected Government of the day. It is there to provide the Government of the day with advice on the formulation of the policies of the Government, to assist in carrying out the decisions of the Government, and to manage and deliver the services for which the Government is responsible.

In a later paragraph he remarked that 'in the determination of policy the civil servant has no constitutional responsibility or role, distinct from  that of the Minister'.  In stressing the personal responsibility civil servants have to their Ministers, and denying the existence of a wide public duty, the note leaves little scope for civil servants whose notions of equity, fairness, democracy and the role of Parliament vary from  that  of  the  Minister  they   currently  serve.   Whilst acknowledging and seeking to make provision for the fact that civil servants may be faced with situations where the legality of the instructions they  have  been  given needs  clarifying, the note offers little comfort to those who feel they are faced with other challenges to the Hennessy genetic code.  Whilst the note might state some of the necessary conditions for preserving the code, I doubt that it states the sufficient conditions.

Civil servants might expect the Civil Service College to play a major role in preserving the code of ethics but there is little evidence in the 1990/91 College Prospectus (Civil Service College 1989) to indicate that this is recognised as an important issue.  Management development programmes designed for public administrators need to place greater emphasis upon ethical issues than would be the case for private sector programmes.

Personal interactions, performance review systems, codes of conduct, management development programmes and notes of guidance will all have a bearing on the preservation of the genetic code. So too will the procedural infrastructure within which public administrators function.  Some of the differences between central and local government are described in an article by David Walker (1990) in which the relative anonymity of the civil servant is portrayed.  This anonymity reflects the secretive process of governmental policy development.  Can we be confident that, subject as they are to many pressures, civil servants feel sufficient direct incentives to respect all aspects of the genetic code in this climate of secrecy?  If we are not so satisfied, do we not need a procedural infrastructure into which such incentives have been consciously inserted? In other words, do we need to institutionalise virtue?

Let us consider the position in local government. The local government officer is a servant of the council as a whole, and not of the majority group. He/she gives advice, both in written reports and orally, in public and is expected to give the same answer to the same question regardless of its origin; from majority or minority party member. Legislation exists to ensure not only that there is fair process but that there is seen to be fair process. So, for example, LEAs must appoint a 'fit person' as their Chief Education Officer, and the Council may not reach a decision on a matter of educational policy before it has been considered by the Education Committee. The composition of an Education Committee is both subject to legislation and approval by the Secretary of State and must contain minority party members. Committee meetings must be held in public; reports which they consider are in the public domain unless containing information of a commercial or personal nature; sources of information on which reports are based must be declared. In this context, despite the inevitability that the ultimate exercise of power will take place in private, the process is regulated in such a way that the actions of the individual officer are sufficiently in the public domain to ensure that there is an incentive to respect the genetic code. Recent events in West Wiltshire provide evidence that an officer with integrity, back-bench politicians asking the right questions, and a vigilant press, have brought to light a situation which, in other circumstances, might have remained hidden (e.g., *The Independent,* 13 January 1990).

Before returning to civil servants, a brief reflection upon managers in the health service is appropriate. They serve authorities whose members are appointed by Ministers and which meet in private. In the absence of the basic features of public accountability, which I suggest are elected bodies and public access to their deliberations, it is difficult to see how this group of public administrators are subject to pressures which will cause them to sustain the genetic code. We have seen the development of many similar arrangements in other areas of the public service in recent years.

During the 1980s the buzzwords in government have been economy, efficiency and effectiveness. We all know what economy means. Spending less money. We have a fairly clear idea what efficiency means. Cutting out practices which contribute nothing to the outcome, achieving the same level of outcome for a reduced level of input, or increasing outcomes for the same level of input. Nothing about the quality of the outcome you notice.

The organisations that central government has employed to pursue the goals of economy and efficiency are easily identified. For local government the Audit Commission, for central government the Efficiency Unit and the National Audit Office. Each has developed its own methodology. The Audit Commission has specialised in comparative studies, drawing on the large number of local authorities to analyse the variations that exist in the unit cost of apparently similar levels of service output. The Efficiency Unit has specialised in 'scrutinies'; in short, sharp, studies conducted within government departments by joint Department/Efficiency Unit teams which set targets for cost reductions. The National Audit Office has specialised in in-depth studies of policy implementation, not questioning the policy itself but examining the procedures used to ensure its execution, particularly its execution within the financial targets set.

As this work has developed it has become clear that the quality of output cannot be ignored. Even if roads can be built within acceptable cost limits, does the fact that the surfaces are already cracking up not matter? (National Audit Office 1989a) So a further catchphrase has been heard; 'Value for Money'; and the third E, effectiveness, has been given attention. Whilst our conceptual grasp of economy and efficiency is quite strong, we have greater difficulties in being precise about effectiveness. It is to do with the quality of output. But how can that quality be measured? If performance measures (e.g., school examination results) are used, do they tell the whole story? Can they be used for comparative purposes? Do they reflect widely held value judgments of the purpose for which the activity whose performance is being measured exists? We have moved from the clarity of the economy/efficiency debate to the complexities of the effectiveness debate with little analysis of the methodologies we use to determine effectiveness.

The Audit Commission, the Efficiency Unit, and the National Audit Office are creatures of the 1980s; quantitative and analytical but working within the framework of existing policy objectives. They have not been, by and large, reflective bodies assisting in the process of policy formulation. The 1970s saw such reflective organisations in action; Royal Commissions to deliberate on major issues of the day, the Central Policy Review Staff (the Think Tank) to give the Cabinet support on cross-departmental issues and to provide a central intelligence capability to 'think the unthinkable'. Where are the equivalent capabilities today? The Central Statistical Office has an important role in the production and publication of information and there is an important debate to be continued on the nature of the information that should be put into the public domain to assist with policy formulation. But the Central Statistical Office does not conduct policy analyses. The political parties have an injection of ideas from their research units and related think tanks but, by definition, these work within political constraints and there is limited opportunity for public debate on their outputs before the government decides whether or not to adopt their thinking. Universities and polytechnics produce work that should inform the policy-making process but there is little evidence that such work is commissioned in a systematic way.

In describing the work of the Audit Commission and National Audit Office in the above terms I do not mean to undervalue their work. Both organisations have demonstrated commendable independence from central government. The Audit Commission, in a study of the response of Local Education Authorities to the decline in secondary school pupil numbers, was critical of the failure of the Department of Education and Science to play its part in effecting school closure and reorganisation proposals put forward by Local Education Authorities (Audit Commission 1986). The National Audit Office's study of the sale of the Rover Group (National Audit Office 1989b) has led to lively exchanges in public. What many of the studies demonstrate is the failure of government to have conducted a thorough analysis of the processes needed to achieve their policy objectives. The Efficiency Unit has, whilst remaining closer to government, made its contribution to management changes through the Next Steps Initiative (Jenkins et.al. 1988). But, as Norman Lewis (1989) has pointed out, there has been little discussion about the wider implications of these changes.

If there is a vacuum in policy analysis, does the experience of the Audit Commission and National Audit Office give any indication of how that vacuum should be filled? The National Audit Office is now firmly established as a creature of Parliament. Its budget is voted by Parliament. Its chief executive, the Comptroller and Auditor General, is appointed by the Chairman of the Public Accounts Committee and the Prime Minister. Its work is presented to the Public Accounts Committee in its role as scrutineer of expenditure authorised by Parliament. The meetings of the Public Accounts Committee are open to the public, which means that the media can, and do, report on its deliberations.

In contrast to the Public Accounts Committees, the other Select Committees have demonstrated less ability to provide Parliament with powerful watchdog capabilities. In a paradoxical way, it has been suggested that their lack of clout helps them to be effective in the sense that being apart from the processing of government business, it is not necessary for governments to smother or 'colonise' them (Drewry 1989). Standing Committees, representing the Parliamentary scrutiny process for legislative proposals, suffer in that, by the time they receive these proposals, the government has fully committed itself to the legislation and is not in a mood for deliberative analysis. The Standing Committees also suffer in being required to consider proposals in the form of Parliamentary Bills which are necessarily written in technical language whose meaning is not always readily apparent.

Let me examine the mechanics of accountability. In management theory, if A is accountable to B, there must be an opportunity for A to understand the terms under which B is delegating authority to take action. This is as true if the initiative for the action comes from A as it is if it comes from B. There must also be a subsequent opportunity for B to review whether A has acted in accordance with these terms.

Constitutional theory states that Ministers in the government are accountable to Parliament. The Public Accounts Committee, with the professional support of the National Audit Office, demonstrates some of the characteristics of the second interaction, reviewing the action taken by Ministers in pursuing action earlier approved by Parliament. There is no doubt in my mind that the other Select Committees need professional support akin to that provided by the National Audit Office if they are to provide an equally robust scrutiny of the implementation of Parliamentary decisions. But where is the earlier process of scrutinising policy proposals? Does anyone seriously believe that the debate on the Queen's Speech confers on the government the considered authority of Parliament to proceed with a legislative programme? What policy analysis papers do MPs have on which to consider proposals? What opportunities exist for MPs to examine the basic information and deductions made by civil servants in the drafting of such policy analysis papers? What opportunities do MPs have to consider alternative deductions that might be drawn by other professionals from the same basic information?

Christopher Hood (1990) has warned of the dangers of 'malversation', an old word for a new form of public corruption. I believe that, by making the policy formulation process more open, we will have a defence against malversation.

I would like to propose that Parliament be given far greater opportunities to deliberate upon the government's legislative proposals before the formal processes of passing legislation through the various Bill stages. To do this, governments should be required to publish, in the form of an extended Green Paper, their policy proposals, setting out the courses of action that they have to choose between, and providing an analysis of the pros and cons of these alternatives. A statutory consultative period should be allowed for comments on the proposals to be made. The comments should be in the public domain and subject, along with the original Green Paper, to an analytical commentary prepared by the staff of a National Office of Policy Analysis, which I shall call NOPA. The appropriate Select Committee of Parliament should then meet to consider the proposals and NOPA's commentary, and be free to cross-examine the Minister and senior civil servants responsible, the officers of NOPA and other key witnesses as judged necessary. The whole process would need to be constrained by set time limits to prevent the excesses of both undue haste and unreasonable delay. There would also need to be provision for urgent legislation to bypass the process, as well as appropriate arrangements for a strictly limited set of issues, relating, for example, to the country's economic and defence interests, to be exempt. We need self-denying legislation equivalent to Gladstone's Exchequer and Audit Department Act of 1866.

In the world of politics power rules, and I accept that a government with sufficient determination would still be able to ensure that its programme reached the statute books. But the process I suggest would make a profound difference to the public exposure of policy analysis. Whilst it is right and proper to call for greater access to public information, that in itself is not enough. Policy analysis needs to be in the public domain too and hence the need for a National Office of Policy Analysis. This would not be dominated by lawyers reaching judgments on the constitutional nature of legislative proposals in the context of a general Bill of Rights or more specific 'rights legislation'. It would have some of the characteristics of the NAO, funded by and accountable to Parliament. A permanent core of staff would lead its work. Others would be seconded from the public and private sectors, from universities and polytechnics to conduct its policy analyses. Its programme of work would be determined by the legislative programme of the day and would provide a documented analysis of policy intentions against which subsequent studies by the NAO of policy implementation would be better informed than at present. As an organisation it would share some of the features of the Standing Advisory Conference proposed by Norman Lewis (1989), but with a narrower focus.

Whilst not undermining the relationship between Ministers and their civil servants and, I hope, the confidence each needs to have in the other, this process would, I suggest, create conditions that would make explicit some aspects of that relationship and so enhance the transmission of the Hennessy genetic code.

Finally, we should ask whether it would produce better legislation. Consider the Education Reform Act of 1988. There is evidence that the need for an Act was widely, if not universally, accepted. There was considerable debate amongst educational administrators about the nature of the Act that was needed. The Act that was passed did not reflect that debate but enacted the wishes of the government of the day with precious little reflective discussion about the consequences of what was being proposed; much of it in the heat of an election campaign. If the reforms had been subject to the process I have proposed, I would suggest that we would have had better legislation, and legislation that would have won greater support amongst educational professionals and the general public.

Let me be bold and indicate what I think would have happened. The National Curriculum would have survived, but the Secretary of State would not have been given such extensive powers over its implementation. Local Financial Management of schools and colleges would have survived, but the simplistic formulae for distributing resources would have been improved upon. Grant maintained schools would not have survived and city technology colleges would not have got beyond the first hurdle in their present form, but might have emerged as more radical post-14 centres of technical excellence. The cynical disdain with which the National Advisory Body's study of Good Management Practice was treated could not have been sustained and there would have been a serious debate about the role of LEAs in the management of post-secondary education. Whilst the Inner London Education Authority would have been subject to major reforms, it would not have been abolished.

You may or may not agree with my analysis of how the Education Reform Act would have turned out had Parliament had the benefit of a NOPA study of Mr. Baker's proposals. At least we would all have been able to relate to a rather more considered process of reform. You may believe that the process I propose would slow Parliamentary procedure too much and lead to inefficient government. I am more interested in effective government. We must not allow ourselves to succumb to pressure to improve the efficiency of an ineffective system. The Hennessy genetic code is about effective government. I urge any of you considering constitutional reform to reflect on the impact your measures will have on the transmission of that code in all parts of the public sector.

---

I should like to acknowledge comments on an early draft of this paper from Peter

Hennessy, Gavin Drewry and Ivor Shelley and bibliographic help from Jane Henderson, RIPA Librarian. The RIPA library and database is available to individual and corporate members of the Institute and contains a wide range of up to date material on Public Administration. Information from RIPA, 3 Birdcage Walk, London SW1H 9JH.

## References

Armstrong, Sir R. (1985) 'The Duties and Responsibilities of Civil Servants in Relation to Ministers', note by the Head of the Home Civil Service, HC 92-II, 1985-6, pp. 7-9.

Audit Commission (1986) *Towards Better Management of Secondary Education*, London, HMSO.

Civil Service College (1989) *'Prospectus 1990 to 1991'*.

Drewry, G. (1989) Memorandum of Evidence to Select Committee on Procedure 1988/89.

Hennessy, P. (1989) *'The Ethics of the Profession'*, GCHQ Memorial Lecture published in the Council for Civil Services Union Bulletin, July 1989.

Hood, C. (1990) *'Beyond the Public Bureaucracy State? Public Administration in the 1990s'*, Inaugural lecture, London School of Economics, January 1990.

Jenkins, K., Caines, K. and Jackson, A. (Efficiency Unit) (1988) *Improving Management in Government: the Next Steps: Report to the Prime Minister,* London, HMSO.

Lewis, N. (1989) 'The Case for a Standing Administrative Conference', *Political Quarterly*, 60, 421-32.

National Audit Office (1989a) *Quality Control of Road and Bridge Construction,* HC 21, 1989-90, London, HMSO.

National Audit Office (1989b) *Department of Trade and Industry: Sale of Rover Group plc to British Aerospace plc*, HC 9, 1989-90, London, HMSO.

Walker, D. (1990) 'Corridors of Power', *Municipal Journal,* 12 January.

# Parliamentary Accountability and Government Control of Information

Maurice Frankel

My starting point is this exchange, from 1979:

> **Mrs Renee Short** asked the **Prime Minister** whether she intends to bring forward legislation to establish a public right of access to official information.
> **The Prime Minister**: No.
> **Mrs Renee Short** asked the Prime Minister if she is satisfied with the current public right of access to official information.
> **The Prime Minister:** Yes. (975 HC Debs, col. 93 (written answer), 4 December 1979)

The economy of words may be quintessentially Mrs Thatcher, but the sentiments are those of all prime ministers. The system of access with which Mrs Thatcher pronounced herself so satisfied depends on Parliament demanding information from ministers. Yet Parliament itself has no specific rights to information: ultimately, all it can do is withdraw support from a government that refuses to answer for its actions. The drastic nature of this sanction guarantees that it will rarely, if ever, be used - which is why governments are so content with it.

Indeed, there is virtually no difference between the present government and its predecessor on this. Both rejected a Freedom of

Information Act on the grounds that it would undermine parliamentary accountability. This is the Labour government in 1979:

> The government cannot accept that a statutory right of access which could affect adversely and fundamentally the accountability to Ministers to parliament is the right course to follow. (Cmnd. 7520)

And this is Mrs Thatcher in 1983:

> Under our constitution, Ministers are accountable to parliament for the work of their departments, and that includes the provision of information. A statutory right of public access would remove this enormously important area of decision-making from parliament and transfer ultimate decisions to the courts ... Ministers' accountability to parliament would be reduced, and parliament itself diminished... In our view the right place for Ministers to answer for their decisions in the essentially 'political' area of information is in parliament. (quoted in Wilson 1984: 134-5)

How do Parliament's 'political' instincts serve us in this area? How insistent is Parliament on its - and our - right to know? The first thing to say is that much of the time Parliament doesn't insist because Parliament is on holiday. In a normal year, Parliament sits for about 170 days (Griffith and Ryle 1989: 182). It is in recess the rest of the time. The formal mechanisms of accountability - debates, questions, select committees - are suspended, and government rules without parliamentary scrutiny of any kind.

Ministers are well aware of the advantages of the recess. Controversial reports have a knack of appearing just as Parliament packs its bags. For example, in 1988, detailed figures for hospital waiting lists were delayed by a full six months - finally appearing on the day Parliament broke up for the summer recess (*The Times*, 30 July 1988). The government's plans for community care were published in a White Paper in November 1989 on the last day of the old parliamentary session. The legislation itself was published just six days later, as the new session began (*The Times*, 14 November 1989; *The Guardian*, 15 November 1989). The timing deprived MPs of the opportunity to question ministers about the proposals. The instant transformation of the White Paper into a Bill meant that the normal period of public consultation was eliminated altogether.

Significantly, it was on an element of this bill that the government, in March 1990, met its first Commons defeat for four years; its instant response was to introduce a 'guillotine' motion, forcing the bill through without further debate (*Daily Telegraph*, 15 March 1990).

That Parliament tolerates such high-handedness at all raises questions about how able, and perhaps more importantly how willing, it is to assert its rights as a body independent of government. The political aspects are of course central to this debate; but the physical limitations under which MPs work should not be overlooked. Nowadays, a significant part of an MP's time is devoted to the problems of individual constituents. An MP with a typical inner city constituency has a 'case load' of about 2,500 cases a year (Lock 1988). This must to some extent be at the expense of other activities. It is not helped by the abysmal facilities. You can still find four MPs sharing a single office in the House of Commons, with their secretaries housed in an entirely different building in the Westminster complex.

Far more significant is the dearth of staff. A 1986 survey found that 40 per cent of MPs had no research assistant. Where MPs had such assistants they usually worked only part-time. Only 18 per cent of MPs had a full time researcher. And doubts were expressed as to whether many 'research assistants' deserved the title at all, since their main activity was the routine collation of information which could just as well have been done by a competent secretary (Cmnd. 131-II: p. 4 and Appendix E, p. 34). Some assistance is available from the House of Commons library, but the average MP operates more or less single-handed. This enormously limits their ability to enquire deeply into anything. Even in an area which is of special interest to an MP he or she may have difficulty keeping up with what the government is *publishing*, let alone think seriously about what may have been concealed, and how to get at it.

Some MPs had begun to make use of student volunteers. But in 1989 the House of Commons limited each MP to a maximum of 3 staff passes. Austin Mitchell MP commented:

> As a result I can't help British students who want to
> see Parliament from the inside and help me at the
> same time. Americans have to hole up in my room
> and be conducted in and out like terrorists. My two
> Grimsby secretaries are unable to spend any time in

> the Commons on their rare visits here unless I'm
> present to shepherd them in and out, take them to the
> toilet, and generally chaperon their movements (*The
> House Magazine*, 8 January 1990).

There are other administrative obstacles. For example the number of
letters that can be taken to the House of Commons by hand for
same-day delivery is limited. The limit is - one! An outside body
cannot get an urgent briefing to an all-party grouping of, say, three MPs
unless there are three letter-carriers to deliver them. If you arrive at
the Commons alone you must choose which of the three MPs is to get
priority. Letters for the other two can only be left if they are stamped
- when they will be re-routed to the Commons Post Office, held up for
24 hours, and delivered with the following day's mail.

Why do MPs tolerate conditions which must make the job of
parliamentary scrutiny so difficult? The sad answer is that some, at
least, do not see scrutiny as part of their job. This is how one
Conservative MP put it:

> The job of a backbencher is not intended to be a
> full-time one.....it is understood that the great
> majority will be there, in Burke's phrase, as
> 'representatives' to support or oppose the
> government, not continually to meddle with it.
> (Dudley Fishburn *The Times,* 20 January 1990)

In normal parliaments the majority of MPs, by definition, are from the
governing party. They may vigorously criticise their own ministers in
private but, unless a policy becomes electorally damaging, will rarely
do so in public. They see their public role as to support the government
and to undermine the opposition's pretensions to replace it. They will
be reluctant to press for information which shows that a policy is flawed
or a blunder has been made. When the opposition tries to highlight the
government's failings, the majority - almost by reflex - may find itself
colluding with the government in covering them up.

MPs, who never cease to think about the next election, are all
too aware that their fate depends on the government's public standing.
Its supporters are certainly not anxious to uncover anything that
threatens the credibility of ministers or undermines the image of a
competent, honest administration. If a mistake has been made they
may seek privately to correct it: if they cannot, they may be content to
see the evidence of such blemishes suppressed.

Moreover, a great number of MPs are themselves actually part of government - and unable to express any public dissent. In March 1990 over a third of all Conservative MPs (130 out of 374) were either ministers or parliamentary private secretaries to ministers.

The great number of ministerial posts, and the frequency of reshuffles, constantly reminds MPs of the prospects for personal advancement. The government whips leave no doubt that it is loyalty, not independence, which will be rewarded. Conservative MP Richard Shepherd has commented:

> We could hand our votes over to the Whips' Office as soon as we come by power of attorney and go away for four years. I can see my hon. Friends the Whips finding this a most agreeable function. It would simplify government. (152 HC Debs., col.136, 2 May 1989)

To put it bluntly, many MPs on the government side see themselves not as a body independent of the Executive but as the ministerial reserves, a pool of potential replacements anxious to demonstrate how suitably they would fill any vacancy. The implications for accountability are disastrous.

Two important qualifications must be recognised. First, cross-party alliances, particularly on select committees, do form and can be effective. But even they cannot force the hand of a minister determined to withhold the facts, and able to rely on partisan support in the full House of Commons. Moreover, the need for consensus may persuade committees to steer clear of controversial inquiries from the outset[1] or to blunt the impact of their reports. Thus the Defence Committee's highly critical reports on the government's conduct during the Westland affair were deliberately published on the day before the summer recess (Drewry 1989).

Second, there are always individual MPs whose public approach is determined by their knowledge of and commitment to the subject, and not by political convenience. But on any issue these are the minority, not least because un-staffed MPs simply cannot develop independent expertise in more than a handful of subjects.

If MPs on the government side begin to take too much of an independent line on legislation, debate is curtailed. The community care legislation has already been mentioned. A further example was the Official Secrets Bill, whose committee stage was taken on the floor of the House of Commons in 1989. On the Bill's first committee day, Conservative MPs were subject to a two-line whip. The mounting

Conservative dissent provoked an immediate change to a three-line whip for the second day and, by day three, a guillotine motion - ensuring the abandonment, without debate or vote, of virtually all remaining amendments. [2]

A guillotine motion itself has to be approved by a majority in Parliament. The fact that the majority so readily assents, when the prime purpose is to prevent them hearing arguments which might convince them, reveals how unconcerned about its own independence, and subservient to the wishes of the government, Parliament can be.

This is apparent too in the ease with which ministers are able to mislead. According to Sir Douglas Wass, former permanent secretary at the Treasury and joint head of the civil service:

> most civil servants would say they have hardly, if ever, come across an instance of a Minister actually lying to Parliament....What is far more common is....the Minister, by judicious presentation and omission, may give an impression to Parliament which is not the impression which would be formed if someone had all the evidence (HC 92, 1985-6: Vol II, p. 42).

The evasion is most obvious in the handling of parliamentary questions. The individual MP can *ask* questions but, as the standard guide to parliamentary procedure put it, 'an answer cannot be insisted upon if the answer be refused by a Minister.' (Gordon 1983: 342)

A brief selection gives the flavour. Ministers may offer some explanation for refusing to answer, but even this is unnecessary:

> **Working Groups and Working Parties**
> Dr. Cunningham: To ask the Secretary of State for the Environment if he will place in the Library papers produced for recent meetings of the (a) new systems working group, (b) rates working party, (c) community charge working group, (d) community charge implementation sub-group and (e) capital programmes working party; and if he will undertake to do so for future meetings of these working groups and working parties.
>
> Mr. Ridley: No. (149 HC Debs., col.92, 13 March 1989)

A common reason for refusing is the cost. There is a particular irony to the response to the following question, given the staggering sums of public money wasted by inefficient military spending:

### Procurement
Mr. Kirkwood: To ask the Secretary of State for Defence if he will publish the details of all procurement projects on which money has been spent in the last five years, but which have not directly resulted in equipment being adopted by the armed services.

Mr. Alan Clark: The information requested could be provided only at disproportionate cost. (160 HC Debs., col. 187 (written answers), 14 November 1989)

Usually, a single reason for refusing to answer is enough. But sometimes the minister drives the point home. When the Minister of State at the Department of Employment was asked how much TV advertising time the Department had purchased from each ITV network, he replied:

Information....in the form requested is not held by my Department, nor is it available centrally through the Central Office of Information and can only be supplied at disproportionate cost. It is also commercially confidential. (153 HC Debs., col. 51 (written answers), 15 May 1989)

A question may be so simple that no respectable grounds for refusing can be found. These can simply be ignored, without obvious signs of ministerial embarrassment. This question required either a straight 'Yes' or 'No':

### Bovine Somatotropin
Dr David Clark: to ask the Minister of Agriculture, Fisheries and Food if he has received any advice or recommendations from his veterinary products committee following appeals by any of the companies involved in the experimental farm trials into the use of bovine somatotropin in cows.

Mr. Donald Thompson: The veterinary products committee provides advice in confidence to my Department at any stage of a product licence application, if appropriate. (146 HC Debs., col. 780 (written answers), 9 February 1989)

A private member's bill introduced early in 1990 by Martyn Jones MP to improve consumer guarantees ran into unexpected opposition from the government, although the sponsor believed it had almost universal support elsewhere. Mr. Jones therefore asked the relevant department to list the organisations which had expressed opposition to the proposals. The Parliamentary Under Secretary of State for Trade and Industry, Mr Eric Forth, replied:

It would be inappropriate to name bodies who have expressed views in confidence. (165 HC Debs., col. 186 (written answers), 16 January 1990)

The following week Mr Jones tabled another question; this time merely asking *how many* organisations had opposed the proposals. Mr. Forth replied:

It would be inappropriate to quantify the bodies involved in the same way as it would be to name them, since their views have been expressed in confidence. (165 HC Debs., col. 506 (written answers), 22 January 1990)

Finally, there is this:

**Parliamentary Answers (Cost)**
Mr Tony Banks: asked the Prime Minister what is the sum above which an answer to a parliamentary question is considered to represent disproportionate cost.

The Prime Minister: It is for Ministers to decide whether to decline to answer a question on grounds of disproportionate cost. Any question likely to cost more than £200 is referred to the responsible Minister before significant cost resources are committed.

> Mr Tony Banks: asked the Prime Minister how many
> questions she has refused to answer since 1979 on the
> grounds of disproportionate costs.
>
> The Prime Minister: This information can be
> supplied only at disproportionate cost. (121 HC
> Debs., cols. 358-9 (written answers), 29 October
> 1987)

Since that time, the cost threshold has been raised to £250.  But
ministers are free to spend unlimited amounts on questions if they want
to.    In  June 1989  the Prime Minister was  asked to list the
government's achievements over the previous ten years.  The reply
covered 34 columns of Hansard, the equivalent of a 90 minute speech.
Its cost, later disclosed, was £4,600. (*The Times*, 14 June 1989)

Of course ministers may also be questioned, by journalists and
broadcasters, outside Parliament.  But here too they contrive to avoid
rigorous cross examination.  Occasionally the broadcasters blow the
whistle  on  a  minister's demands.  This is how the Thames TV
consumer programme 'For What It's Worth' prefaced an item about
social security:

> As part of our film we wanted to interview the Social
> Security Minister Nicholas Scott.  He said he would
> speak to us only if he was given all our questions in
> advance and provided he was given a written synopsis
> of the points made by all our other interviewees.
> What's more he insisted that his interview be
> un-edited and that none of the other interviewers be
> allowed to comment on anything he said.  So it was
> under these reporting restrictions that I spoke to him
> earlier today.  (Broadcast on 5 December 1989)

In a self-respecting democracy the only response to these many forms
of manipulation must surely be to assert that our right to know is
fundamental, and too important to be abused in this way.  Part of the
answer is a Freedom of Information Act.

Many countries have already adopted such laws, including the
USA, Australia, Canada, New Zealand, Sweden, Norway, Holland,
Denmark and France.  The law takes the form of a general right of
access to government information, available to any citizen.  A series of
exemptions allow particular classes of information to be withheld.

Typically these cover disclosures which would be harmful to defence, foreign relations, national security or law enforcement: or which would jeopardise personal privacy or trade secrets. Most countries also exempt the policy advice of officials. Government claims for exemption can be challenged by appeal to the court or, in some countries, an independent commissioner.

Nothing in this approach is incompatible with our system of government. Parliament itself would define the exemptions, and be free to revise them (as Australia has done, twice) in the light of experience. Indeed, on a modest scale we already have such laws, the most obvious example being the Data Protection Act 1984. The Act, which in its structure and exemptions is remarkably similar to a freedom of information act, gives individuals the right to see computer files held on them, by government as well as others.

One of the first beneficiaries under FOI would be Parliament. MPs themselves could use the Act, and they would benefit from the more informed news coverage and broader public debate resulting from its use by others.

The impressive variety of uses to which the US Freedom of Information Act has been put has been well-documented (Hendricks 1982). It is used by individuals seeking government records held on them to ensure that they are not being denied benefits through error or arbitrary action. Consumer and environmental groups constantly uncover safety hazards known to but ignored by government inspectors; companies use it to protect themselves against discrimination in the allocation of contracts or the enforcement of standards; accident victims use it to help prepare for litigation; historians, authors, journalists, pressure groups from the left and right all rely on it, and it has produced a steady stream of revelations about the improper and wasteful use of government funds.

In both Australia and Canada ministers have been forced to resign after freedom of information disclosures revealed improprieties (Hazell 1989). One celebrated disclosure under the Australian Act forced the cancellation of an expensive military project for the establishment of a tank training area after internal documents revealed that the site was totally unsuitable for the purpose. The amount saved - more than £250 million - represented nearly 40 times the annual cost of the Australian FOI Act.

In both Australia and Canada FOI currently costs just under £7 million per year (Hazell 1989). To put this in context, in the UK we currently spend £62 million a year on military bands (*The*

*Independent*, 14 September 1989), and nearly £200 million a year on government publicity (HC 46 1989-90: p. 2).

The prospects for FOI in Britain depend on a change of government. Both Labour and the Liberal Democrats are committed to introducing a Freedom of Information Act; the reform was also promised in the Labour and Alliance 1987 election manifestos.

Will the promise be kept? The attractions of freedom of information to an opposition party quickly wear off when it arrives in government. The 1974 Labour election manifesto promised FOI, but the Labour government went on to reject the reform (Cmnd. 7520).

The present signs do not suggest that this scenario will be repeated. The 1974 commitment was barely mentioned by Labour's leadership at the time, and there is little evidence that most of them understood, let alone personally endorsed, the proposal. The present Labour opposition has repeatedly committed itself to the reform, and key figures from the leader of the party down have put their own personal support unequivocally on the record. Moreover, in the climate of 1974 FOI was a radical and unknown prospect, seen only in countries - such as the USA and Sweden - with un-British systems of government. FOI now is a well tested reform, successfully implemented in countries such as Australia and Canada with Westminster-style parliaments.

On the other hand, in a highly confrontational Parliament ministers must be tempted to use every advantage of office to deny their opponents ammunition. A fresh set of ministers, having suffered in opposition so long, will not enjoy giving up the unrivalled advantage which their new control of information offers. And the attraction of being able to conceal one's errors grows with the number of errors made. If the new reform is not introduced quickly there will be doubts whether it will come at all.

## Notes

1. 'We have noted again and again the stress on the need for consensus within a committee if its work was to achieve anything, and that this imperative has on occasion severely limited a committee's conception of its objective, sometimes becoming the principal objective itself' (Giddings 1989: 369).
2. The first committee day was 25 January 1989; the second was 2 February 1989; the guillotine motion was moved on 13 February 1989.

## References

Drewry, G. (1989) 'The Committees since 1983' in G. Drewry (ed.), *The New Select Committees*, Oxford, Clarendon Press.

Giddings, P. (1989) 'What has been Achieved?' in G. Drewry (ed.), *The New Select Committees,* Oxford, Clarendon Press.

Gordon, Sir. C. (ed.) (1983) *Erskine May's Treatise on the Law, Privileges, Proceedings and Usage of Parliament*, 20th edition, London, Butterworths.

Griffith, J.A.G. and Ryle, M. (1989) *Parliament: Functions, Practice* and *Procedures,* London, Sweet and Maxwell.

Hazell, R. (1989) 'Freedom of Information in Australia, Canada and New Zealand', *Public Administration*, 67, 189-210.

Hendricks, E. (1982) *Former Secrets: Government Records made Public through the Freedom of Information Act*, Washington, DC, Campaign for Political Rights.

Lock, G. (1988) 'Information for Parliament' in M. Ryle and P.G. Richards (eds.), *The Commons under Scrutiny*, London Routledge.

Wilson, D. (ed.) (1984) *The Secrets File*, London, Heinemann.

# The Sovereignty of Parliament and the Scottish Question

Bernard Crick

'I am a citizen of a state with no agreed colloquial name', I began a recent essay in the *Irish Review* (Crick 1988). I reflected on the difficulty we Brits (to use an Aussie expletive now favoured by both persuasions in Northern Ireland - and to them both Scots and Welsh are 'Brits' too) have in responding to the peremptory 'Nationality?' of a foreign hotel register. Few people, I've observed, write 'British'. Most mistakenly take the question literally, not as asking for one's legal citizenship. The question was framed, not for us Ukanians, but for those in happy lands where one nation is one state: or so it is believed. The word 'British' doesn't, to paraphrase Catullus, 'warm the blood like wine', as 'English' can, and 'Scottish', 'Welsh' and 'Irish'. 'British is best' sounds to my ear either commercial or evasive of the question of identity. Those who write 'citizen of the United Kingdom' invariably turn out to be Ulster Loyalists, and perhaps a few aggressive and pedantic Scottish Tories.

The majority, of course, write 'English' for the good enough reason that they are English. But some do so in the mistaken belief that 'English' is the adjective corresponding to 'citizen of the United Kingdom of Great Britain and Northern Ireland'. The full title of the Union is a mouthful. One needs a sense of history to digest it. But many Englishmen and women, high and low, now seem to have lost just such a sense of history, and are only left with a vague, warm, nostalgic and evasive mental mist called 'English heritage'. Even to speak of 'the Union' would risk, in some contexts, sounding as if one was either anti-Catholic or opposed to a Parliament in Scotland. But it is too true a description of the foundations of our modern constitution to surrender to partisan rhetoric. I am a modern democratic socialist, but if ever popular political banquets came back in fashion, I would lift my glass, like an eighteenth century Whig, and drink 'to the Union, God bless it' (although perhaps not after 1798 and 1800 in company who favoured the suppression of the Parliament of Ireland).

A personal explanation is needed. I am a deliberate immigrant in Scotland because I came to love the country. But so different is the culture, and so strong my Englishness, that however Scottish my political and constitutional views have become (for good reasons, as I'll seek to convince you), I am now, to be honest, too old to believe that I'll ever think of myself or be thought of as Scottish, as my student friends in the late 1940's, whose Jewish parents had sent them from Germany as children, were already English. For at the heart of the matter there is, what Mrs. Thatcher cannot grasp, or only grasp in an English context, national feeling, indeed nationalism. But nationalism does not necessarily imply separatism, nor that for each nation there must be a state.[1] There are multi-national states and there are also many areas of the world (we need look no further than Ireland, or Israel/Palestine or South Africa) where nationalism is part of the problem, not of any 'solution'. The word 'resolution' is usually better.

Most Scots, like most Welsh, have an intense sense of dual identity, and for most purposes live with it comfortably, indeed find an enhanced quality of life in being able to live in two worlds, enjoy two cultures and their hybrids. But they perceive this, of course (except in mixed marriages), as being Scottish and British, not Scottish and English. The late John Mackintosh, MP, put it well:

> The case for devolution explicitly limits political change to the level which allows self awareness but excludes nationalist extremism. It keeps Scotland in the United Kingdom on the explicit grounds that Scots have a dual nationality; they are English as well as Scottish. Though this does not rule out the less pleasant forms of nationalism, it prevents the practical expression of any Scottish national feeling in the form of hostility to the English. (Mackintosh 1977)

So much of the sub-text of Scottish constitutional nationalism is, of course, an implicit if seldom stated comparison with Northern Ireland. But that does depend on how both sides behave. The provocations of the 1960s and 1970s, when Mackintosh wrote, were of a kind more easily discounted or overcome than the abrasive, confrontational English politics of the 1980s.

> [There are] ...two ways in which one can feel Scottish and I think I have experienced both. One ... is to feel a resentment against the assumptions of superiority, of absolute standards, so evident in the older English universities, in London media circles, among Whitehall civil servants and so on. The other, when one has been in and through all these groups and their activities, is to be reasonably confident that the best of what is done in Scotland and by Scots is as good as anything these guardians of proper standards can produce. (Drucker 1982: 149)

The difficulty is that this reasonable sense of dual identity is not shared by most of the English, and that it also depends on historically sensitive behaviour by the English towards the other nations in the Union; on their not misusing the quantum of power that lies all too easily to hand, both in the institutions and the doctrines of the states.

This power has been abused (or so most people in Scotland think) and a constitutional crisis is likely to result, however much of this is dismissed south of the border due to the appalling lack of interest in and under-reporting of Scotland even in the quality London press and broadcasting media. Editors and political writers read the press wires for events in foreign countries, but here they think they know already. After all, they go to Scotland on holiday, sometimes, or to the borders for winter weekend breaks. But their knowledge is, in fact, a knowledge of political opinion in London from daily talk with people in London. They meet Scottish Labour and SLD MPs, of course, but they think they are exaggerating; and the Scots go home at weekends and in the recess, so are not on the scene. How else can one explain that the last Mori Polls in *The Scotsman* (19 September 1989) went unreported in the London press although they showed 34 per cent favouring independence, 49 per cent for 'Home Rule' (a subsidiary Parliament but with substantial and residual powers including taxation), and only 15 per cent favouring 'no change' with an incredibly low 2 per cent with 'no opinion'. Of course, put to the test of a referendum campaign, say, as in 1979, the 'no change' or misnamed

'Unionist' note would undoubtedly increase;  but the figures, and the intensity of feeling, are *far greater* than ten years ago (Kellas 1989). Thatcherism has fanned the fire but the fire never went out.  It is only that politicians and their captive audience of political writers are mainly impressed by events, not trends and tendencies.

An event brought the Scottish Parliamentary Labour Party out of a luke-warm and divided support for 1978 style devolution into an apparently unequivocal enthusiasm for Home Rule;  viz. the Govan by-election when Jim Sillars for the SNP destroyed an impregnable 19,000 Labour majority.  Their rank and file had already reached the same position.  The Campaign for a Scottish Assembly, a body of great influence in Scotland, virtually unreported south of the border, had set up a committee which produced what is likely in future to be regarded as a classic statement of the Scottish political mind, *A Claim of Right for Scotland* (Campaign for a Scottish Assembly 1988).  Leave aside, for the moment, some rather old-fashioned romantic history picturing the Act or Treaty of Union as a great betrayal (rather than as a hard bargain, grudgingly conceded), and a dubious claim for a dubious doctrine - that Scottish constitutional law embodied a belief in 'the sovereignty of the people'.   Nonetheless the truculent moderation of its argument that the Scottish people have a right to choose gained wide assent.  The device for the choosing was to be a Constitutional Convention and the implication was that neither a Convention nor a referendum was likely to show a separatist majority but rather one for Home Rule, or in effect, if not in name, for a federal system.  Certainly it swept opinion in the Constituency Labour Parties and the Scottish TUC.  The Liberals or the SLD were already in that position, and had been since the 1900s.

The SNP refused to commit itself to a majority report, understandably favouring a referendum on the three obvious broad alternatives (independence, 'devolution', no change)  before a proposal was drafted;  so they withdrew, hoping to leave Labour holding the baby and being punished for not being able to do anything with it. Post-Govan euphoria helped their decision. But their standing in the polls declined almost at once (Crick 1989). The true message of Govan  was not easy for either of  the two main Scottish parties;  that the electorate is extremely volatile and will punish drastically either party if they do not appear (as depth interviews reveal) 'to be doing enough for Scotland'.  Labour was punished at Govan as was the SNP for refusing to join the Convention.  But this means that the Scottish Labour Party have to encourage a radical report and to fight for it. And they also have to appear as leaders of a Scottish national movement, not just a Labour Party whose status is simply that of a regional organisation of the national (London) Labour Party. This means, in practice, that the small SLD tail at the Convention can wag the big Labour dog on the issue of proportional representation (whatever Mr. Kinnock and Mr. Hattersley might want), just as collectively the Scottish Labour MPs would have a victorious Mr. Kinnock in 1992 in much the same position that Parnell had Gladstone in the 1880s.

Forgive this raw and speculative politics in a symposium on constitutional law. But I am making the unlikely point that the whole Scottish tail is likely to wag the English dog and force on constitutional reform that might otherwise simply remain what Mr. Kinnock called the Charter 88 movement, an affair of the 'chattering classes'. But Charter 88 is itself (if one of its early signators may cheerfully confess) a symptom quite as much as a cause. Several books and many articles and editorials, at almost all levels, had already been raising issues of Bills of Rights, electoral reform, freedom of information, indeed of the possible need for comprehensive constitutional reform, possibly a written constitution, as if the old informal, conventional constitutional order was breaking down.[2]

So I want to consider the consequences of *A Claim of Right* for the constitution of the United Kingdom as a whole. It does, indeed, call into question the whole character of the constitutional settlement that followed 1688 and 1707. This is precisely why many English Conservatives so vehemently oppose any Devolution or Home Rule, as well as why most Scots and a growing minority of English (I mean a probable majority of those who think about constitutional issues at all) now favour it. The traditional response of English politicians was to make conciliatory gestures and to search for compromise or compensatory positions; either Burke's great virtue of 'prudence' or Macmillan's or Wilson's soft fudge. But Margaret Thatcher practices a melodramatic either-or confrontationalism; the Union (God bless it!) or separation and the break-up of the United Kingdom which, without further argument, she seems to equate with disorder and anarchy; having, presumably, never heard of Austria. She dismissed any middle ground whatever in her Glasgow speech of 4 February 1989.

> This Government believes in devolution to the individual citizen, a devolution now being practised in the United Kingdom ... This Government remains committed to the Union, as committed as ever.

In the words of one of her most assiduous supporters or courtiers, Bill Walker, MP: 'It is now time our party called for a referendum and put to the people of Scotland a straight question, "Do you want to remain part of the United Kingdom and Great Britain - Yes or No?"' (*The Scotsman,* 5 February 1989). However, in missing the main point and excluding all majority middle ground, they splendidly illuminate the constitutional issue and dilemma, as well as the fallacy of the excluded middle.

### An Historical Excursus

Let us go back to the beginning, to the Act or Treaty of Union of 1707: part of the living memory of Scotland and just one part of the dead past in England. The very name and nature of it is still in dispute. The canny Scottish Lords of Appeal have never been drawn into judgment in any case meant to test whether alleged breaches of the Treaty of Union by Act of Parliament could be illegal. The response of English judges would be more robust and less equivocal: that Parliament has absolute power to legislate on anything it chooses. Therefore no Parliament can be bound by the Acts of its predecessors, however solemn; so the Act or Treaty of Union is simply an ordinary enactment, and even if it was a treaty, treaty obligations can be overridden by future enactments of Parliament, presumably even the Treaty of Rome.

The 16th edition of Sir Erskine May's *Treatise on the Law ... of Parliament* intones:

> The constitution has assigned no limits to the authority of Parliament over all matters and persons within its jurisdiction. A law may be unjust and contrary to the sound principles of government; but Parliament is not controlled in its discretion, and when it errs, its errors can only be corrected by itself. To adopt the words of Sir Edward Coke (1552-1634), the power of Parliament 'is so transcendent and absolute, as it cannot be confined either for causes or for persons within any bounds'.

But this was never as clear as it sounded. Coke was not an intransigent Parliament-man against the Crown. He held that the King had a veto, should sometimes use it, so that the 'transcendent and absolute' power of Parliament was only when the King and Parliament acted together, as in the royal assent to make Bills into Acts. Further Coke explicitly, if somewhat vaguely, believed that there were 'laws of God and of nature' which Parliament could not override, as also some aspects 'of the Ancient Constitution'. So neither good causes, the authority of persons, nor of Parliament itself could override these things. 'Transcendent power' or sovereignty is not always quite what it sounds (see Pocock 1957, 1972).

Practical men of both kingdoms in 1688 and 1707 saw the new abstract doctrine of parliamentary sovereignty as a gigantic bluff (a Leviathan indeed) to maintain order, or in specific terms to ensure the Protestant succession and the end of religious and dynastic civil war, to ensure the predominancy of Parliament over the Crown, and to maintain the unity of the United Kingdom. Power was to be checked and balanced within Parliament, but if divided among the kingdoms, even under one Crown, was to risk anarchy. And men felt that they had come close to 'anarchy' or perpetual civil war in all three kingdoms. Yet every man of affairs in Scotland and England knew that the claim to absolute power was a legal fiction tempered by political reality and mediated by skilled statecraft, sometimes by good or ill fortune.[3]

Did prudence or corruption predominate in the last debates of the old Scottish Parliament? *The Claim of Right* is still coloured by an old romantic nationalist view of history, in a specific nineteenth century form: that a Parliament must embody the life of a nation. 'The nation was not conquered', they say, 'but it did not freely agree to the Union of Parliaments in 1707' (para. 2.5). Certainly there was bribery and corruption in Edinburgh, just as there was in Westminster, to get the Bill through the English House of Lords with the Bishops in uproar. Yet modern historians suggest that most Scots believed that a hard bargain had been driven. 'The matters on which the Treaty guaranteed the Scotts their own institutions and policies represented the bulk of civil life and government at the time; the Church, the Law and Education' (para. 2.6). Nor should we forget commercial union and military security against the Highlands; vastly important and urgent matters. Then again, it is well to remember that Parliament itself was not as respected at the time as it became in legend. True, 'the nation' was not consulted, but nations never were until modern democratic times, and only then most rarely. Much public opinion of the day saw Parliament not as the national institution and the nation's pride but as a corrupt entity mainly serving the interests of the landowning class. But there was a national institution in which the middle classes and the people took pride; the Church of Scotland itself; the Kirk. By the standards of the time it was a remarkably representative institution, so that at least 'the elect' proceeded by elections. The elected Church Assembly had at least as strong a claim to be seen as the national institution as the Parliament.[4] That is why its establishment was so bitterly fought in the English Upper Chamber.

It was not the case that Scotland suddenly became directly governed by England, but that what government there was, which (leaving aside trade and foreign affairs) was mainly local government, remained in the hands of the Kirk and the legal profession. Indeed with the growth of the modern Scottish Office, Scotland still exhibits an astonishing spectacle of almost complete administrative devolution, and one, moreover, mainly in Scottish hands. English migrants have recently come to dominate some Scottish universities and to penetrate business and the arts to an unprecedented degree - what some call 'the Englishing of Scotland'. But the civil service remains almost wholly a native preserve, and that is, of course, the minimum case for a representative institution in Scotland: that all this existing machinery should be subject to democratic control. What happened was less that Scotland has suffered from having, in an aberrant, epochal and regrettable moment, 'lost' its Parliament, but that the established church it gained gradually lost its dominance over the nation's life and its role as the national institution.

Scotland is full of what the eighteenth century called 'peculiar institutions' but it now lacks an elected national institution. Therefore the commonsense argument is for some form of subsidiary Parliament. But it is not a wholly rational or a commonsense matter. On the one hand, there is nationalism; Scotland is a unique culture and has its own history. It is not a meccano set of institutional arrangements that can be adjusted into the 'greatest happiness' equilibrium position; and on the other hand there is what I call the English ideology of parliamentary sovereignty. It may have outlived its usefulness, but it has left behind deep fears that the creation of any national representative institution in Scotland will lead to the breakup of the United Kingdom.

The English ideology of parliamentary sovereignty arose because from the end of the seventeenth century right up until the Government of Ireland Act 1920, the major business of British politics was holding the United Kingdom together (Pocock 1975, Crick 1982). The presupposition to all activities is often, R.G. Collingwood argued in his *The Idea of History*, the most difficult to grasp and re-imagine. Churchill's generation was the last, even after the formation of the Irish Free State, to have had the history and mythology of this at their fingertips. They did not always succeed, as the Irish rebellion showed, but they knew they had to try, and it was part of 'the Great Game', not just the overseas Empire. Irish historians once painted a lurid canvas of continuous coercion, but their modern successors paint a more complex picture in somewhat softer colours. Firstly, they see the culture, commerce and politics of Britain and Ireland as inextricably intermingled, quite apart from claims of right and justice, and, secondly, they see British policy in the nineteenth century reactive more than settled, as alternating spasms of coercion and conciliation. And these spasms did not always follow change of office between Whig or Tory, Liberal or Conservative.

Scotland was once almost as worrying to the English as Ireland. Memories of 'the 45' lived long. A barbarian army had got as far south as Derby. Famously few English Jacobites rallied to the cause but even more interestingly the county militias proved useless. The gentry did not spring to horse in the numbers they did a century before, but sat back and waited for the small professional army to recover position. The depth of the scare, amongst Scottish unionists not least, is reflected in the savagery of the reprisals. When in 1780, in desperate need of recruits in the unpopular American War, the Government lifted some proscriptions on Catholics to enable the recruitment of Highlanders (the Gurkhas of the first British Empire), it provoked the Gordon Riots in London; anti-Catholic and xenophobic. The fear of these, as shown in two novels of Dickens, echoed into the next century.

The maintainance of law and order and the preservation of the Union were inseparable concepts to both the English and Scottish political classes of that time. After the wars, the old memories and fears were still strong enough for the Government to feel the need to play cards from the other hand: conciliation. There was the ludicrous state charade of George IV's visit to Edinburgh produced by Sir Walter Scott and commissioned by the Cabinet. Only for political necessity did the dropsical Prinny wear the kilt that immortal once. And in the next reign the young Queen was persuaded by Melbourne, at first reluctantly, of the desirability of spending 'an appreciable part of the year in Scotland'. Luckily she liked it. And at that time there was virtually a state cult of Celtic song, poetry and dance. Victoria's children wore tartan plaid and the children of a Viceroy of Ireland wore the green. It was later called 'cultural politics' in other contexts, but it was not then an insensitive and centralising imposition of southern English culture and values (Prebble 1988).

By the last quarter of the nineteenth century any residual English fears that Scotland might become Ireland had vanished. Yet this very time saw the creation of the office of Secretary for Scotland in 1885 and the beginning of the gradual process which led to the modern Scottish Office in Edinburgh. This was, once again, an instinctive, almost routine, English conciliatory politics, triggered more by dubious analogies with Ireland than by actual threats or immediate pressures in

Scotland. Although there was a Scottish Home Rule Association from the 1880s, its influence appears to have been minimal. Indeed, when Liberal leaders in 1910 and 1911 began to talk of 'Home Rule All Round', and Asquith discussed in Cabinet whether to bring in one Bill, or to take the difficult or the easy one first, again the impetus was analogy with Ireland. A pre-emptive or reflex action rather than something dictated by the political power of the Scottish Home Rule movement. Also many ministers of the day, not just thinkers, were coming round to the federalist position of Gladstone's *The Irish Question* pamphlet of 1886. They were beginning to see the drawbacks in 'sovereignty of Parliament' and the constitutionless constitution it entailed. They were influenced by Canadian and Australian experience, American of course, and more immediately by the federal settlement in South Africa after the Boer War. A few Tories even played with ideas of an Imperial federation. Only the Great War brought an end to such speculations, as to much else (Coupland 1954).

The older English ruling class actually knew the component parts of the United Kingdom. 'Absentee landlords' is somewhat of a nationalist myth, as Roy Foster (1988) has recently argued, since most English landowners in Ireland and Scotland were also frequently absent from their English estates. Life was a round between 'town', 'country' and Argyll or Galway. Indeed their families intermarried with local landowning families who almost always owned more land than the 'absentees'. Perhaps the basic political problem is that we now have a generation of English Conservatives in power, not just the Prime Minister, to whom all this is a closed book and whose ignorance about 'the other nations' is monumental. Practical politicians, after all, learn mainly from experience; a credo which was part of the creed of older English Conservatives. Now they have all become liberals, an ideology in which one learns only by doing. This is now a political failing because they cannot take anything seriously that has not been part of their immediate suburban or, at the best, trans-Atlantic experience. Burke once wrote 'An Appeal From the New to the Old Whigs'. Perhaps this essay should be called 'An Appeal From the Old to the New Tories'.

Enough of the old guard were left, however, for the party to change its rigid ways in one important area where the going was hard and obviously most un-English. Since 1980 some very unlikely Northern Ireland Office ministers have worked the subject up, talked to the right people, got quite a feel for the ground, and have done, in the circumstances, reasonably well. And things inherently inimical and contrary to the British Constitution suddenly become possible, indeed necessary: statutory referenda, power-sharing, proportional representation and even 'conditional sovereignty'. The Anglo-Irish Agreement of 1985 stated:

> The two Governments ... declare that if, in the future a majority of the people of Northern Ireland clearly wish for and formally consent to the establishment of a United Ireland, they will introduce and support in their respective Parliaments legislation to give effect to that wish.

Such language and provision for such a poll or referendum was already in the Northern Ireland Constitution Act of 1973 (Hadden and Boyle 1989, Crick 1986). It should give heart to the SNP.

Why cannot this flexible attitude to the Union be extended to Scotland and Wales, though a majority of Scots and Welsh might wish to vote for something different? The answer must be that while most Conservatives are firm that Northern Ireland is part of the United Kingdom, it is sufficiently different for its membership not to be absolute but conditional on the wishes of even a bare majority of its inhabitants. Yet when devolution proposals are suggested for Scotland, it is somehow thought that her membership of the United Kingdom is unconditionally mandatory, even to the extent of denying it a devolved Parliament of the sort already on offer to Northern Ireland. English Conservatives must somehow believe that the Scots are not merely British but are somehow 'really' English, whereas even Loyalist Ulstermen are quite plainly not. Or does the willingness to take seriously another national identity within the United Kingdom need the unhappy stimulant of civil disobedience or violence?

The concept of sovereignty itself is a great obstacle to empathy and imagination in the English political mind. 'Our direct concern is with Scotland only', began *A Claim of Right,* 'but the failure to provide good government for Scotland is a product not merely of faulty British policy in relation to Scotland, but of fundamental flaws in the British constitution' (para. 1.2).

The wide acceptance of the doctrine of the sovereignty of Parliament only took place in the mid-eighteenth century. Previously, the English constitution had been held to be a balance of traditional powers of King, Lords and Commons, just as in Scotland through the Three Estates, though the precise balance and composition of them was always disputed. The new doctrine gained favour in reaction to what was perceived as the intolerable political instability of the previous century and the practical business of holding the three kingdoms together under one Crown. The powers of the monarch ceased to be personal and became 'the Crown' as 'King-in-Parliament', the Prime Minister eventually exercising those powers for so long as he or she could make and keep a majority.

Blackstone set down the classic statement of the doctrine in his *Commentaries on the Laws of England* (1765-69):

> Parliament has sovereign and uncontrollable authority in the making, confirming, enlarging, restraining, abrogating, repealing, reviving and expounding of laws concerning matters of all possible denominations ... this being the place where that absolute despotic power, which must in all governments reside somewhere, is entrusted by the constitution of these kingdoms ... It can change and create afresh even the constitution of the kingdom and of Parliaments themselves; as was done by the Act of Union (with Scotland) and the several statutes for triennial and septennial elections. It can, in short, do everything that is not naturally impossible.
> (Quoted and discussed in Barker 1945: Ch. 5)

His sweeping assertion that all government needed 'absolute despotic power' did not go unchallenged. The young Jeremy Bentham mocked Blackstone in his own first book, *A Fragment on Government* of 1776: 'did the Switzers and Germans then lack government?' But to most English Tories the federal American Constitution of 1787 was to seem, if not a logical impossibility, at least inherently unstable for seeking to check, balance, divide and restrain sovereignty. Not that Blackstone or any serious politician thought that this 'despotic power' would be used regularly. It was an ultimate restraint to prevent others exercising coercive power with public authority. Sovereign power must be exercised with prudence. Even so, it is worth noting that the parliamentary debates over the repeal of the Stamp Act in 1766 show that some still took Coke's view that there were limits, other than practical limits, on parliamentary sovereignty. Taxation, then and now, roused deep passions. Could the Americans be taxed if they were not represented in Parliament, except by their own provincial assemblies? One earnest Member agonised:

> .... two opinions, both equally true (though carrying a
> formal contradiction), were set before us. The one,

that in all free countries none can be taxed, but by
himself or representative. The other that there never
was any country since the Creation where there was
not somewhere lodged, for the superintendancy of
the whole, one supreme legislative authority,
controlling, directing and governing the whole.[5]

The director of the Seven Years War himself, William Pitt, had no
doubts, and dragged himself in his last illness to protest in Parliament:

... that this Kingdom has no right to lay a tax upon the
colonies, to be sovereign and supreme in every
circumstance of government whatsoever. They are
the subjects of this kingdom, equally entitled with
yourselves to all the natural rights of mankind and the
peculiar privileges of Englishmen.... the Americans
are the sons not the bastards of England. Taxation is
no part of the governing or legislative power. The
taxes are a voluntary gift and grant of the Commons
alone.... Here I would draw the line.[6]

He was, however, in the minority, and many dismissed his argument as
'patriotic' rabble-rousing. Nonetheless, in repealing the Stamp Act
on prudential grounds, the King's Ministers found it necessary to push
the Declaratory Act (1766) through Parliament which stated that
Parliament had absolute power to legislate on any subject whatever
respecting any British subject. It was passed, but only narrowly. Many
would have preferred to hedge the issue. Edmund Burke in his
subsequent great speeches on *Conciliation with America* and on
*American Taxation* was to rail at Lord North's claim that the American
refusal to pay taxes threatened the sovereignty of Parliament. Do not
ask, he said, 'whether you have a right to make them miserable, have
you not rather an interest to make them happy?':

...if intemperately, unwisely, fatally, you sophisticate
and poison the very source of government, by urging
subtle deductions and consequences odious to those
you govern, from the unlimited and illimitable nature
of supreme sovereignty, you will teach them by these
means to call that sovereignty itself into question.
(Burke 1908)

And that was precisely what happened, and could happen again now.

By opposing all concessions and slamming the door on any discussions of change (even within her own party in Scotland), Margaret Thatcher, very like Lord North (or his master), has raised the stakes dramatically and foolishly. Some will think that she has, indeed, strengthened the hands and hearts of separatist nationalists in Scotland. Perhaps. But I think it more likely that her intransigence has swept mere devolution off the agenda and is almost overnight turning devolutionists into federalists in the Scottish Labour Party. The whole constitution of the United Kingdom is now called into question, and there is no secure way forward for Scotland unless it is. Unhappily while Mrs Thatcher has turned her back on Burke, Labour's leaders still echo him. They plead for and rely upon a prudence which is not there. They seek vigorously, like Mr Hattersley, to fudge the sovereignty issue. They can sound equally magnificent, perhaps, but the impact could prove equally futile. Like Burke, they are hedging the fundamental issue. For Burke, as is clear in the above passage, was not attacking sovereignty as such, but its imprudent abuse in bad policies. Labour's present leaders also believe in 'unlimited and supreme... sovereignty' but want it in their own good hands, and might, indeed, if it falls to them, exercise it more prudently and benignly. However, by the time Burke spoke it was too late. The Americans did not just want better treatment, they wanted constitutional guarantees for a defined area of self-government. They were not prepared to wait for a more friendly government, and to trust for restraint, like good English politicians, to friendship alone. So also the Scots. Those in London who take Scotland seriously at all continue to talk of the demand for devolution. So do many in Scotland, for want of a better concept, though 'Home Rule' is catching on. But most Scots now want, as the Constitutional Convention will almost certainly demand, devolution with entrenched powers. And as we all know, that is impossible in the present traditional, informal, conventional and unwritten constitution.

### The Constitution in Ferment

It used to be argued, in private by the main draughtsman of the Scotland Act of 1978 before he retired from the Scottish Office, that the details of the 1978 Bill were of secondary importance. Many pro-devolutionists at the time shared this view and were prepared to obtain an Assembly of some kind and to assume that as its authority grew, so new powers would be added, or simply assumed. Such a process would be politically, even if not legally, irreversible. But Jim Ross has recently seen the catch in the Burkean argument for prudence. His article 'A Fond Farewell to Devolution' (Ross 1988) has had considerable effect on the Scottish reformers, not least in the committees of the Convention.

Ross simply argued that in 1978 'we were innocent enough' to suppose that future Ministers would not dare withdraw powers once granted. 'We now know better. We used to think that Governments under the British constitution were fussy and interfering but not fundamentally undemocratic. We now know that the British constitution is inherently authoritarian and is quite capable of spawning a Government to match.' So he concludes that the objective must be, however politically difficult, a constitutionally protected Scottish Parliament, such that only by some special and difficult procedure could Parliament wind it up, change its powers or reduce its funding.

In 1981, with the events of 1979 very much in mind, I remember offering this question to the University of London School Examination Board: '"Devolution was a concept invented by Harold Wilson to obscure the hitherto clear distinction between local government and federalism". Explain and discuss.' The teacher-assessors understandably threw it out as too difficult for the English candidates. But it would have been fully comprehensible, then and now, to any Scottish sixth-former.

*The Claim of Right* sees the English constitution as a barrier to Scottish rights to a national representative institution. But it is now widely canvassed, as never before (except within the old Liberal Party for most of this century!) that the constitution is an obstacle to all our British civil liberties. The lack of restraint upon government has reached epic proportions.

*The Political Quarterly*, a journal not famous for sensationalism, had a recent issue on 'Is Britain Becoming Authoritarian?' with Wyn Grant (1989) writing comprehensively of 'The Erosion of Intermediary Institutions'. There is no need to labour the point that many political thinkers have seen intermediary institutions as essential conditions for liberty. But Wyn Grant sombrely pointed out that the erosion is not simply a product of Thatcher's deliberate policies, but follows from another strong tradition, rooted in the classical economists, which sees any intermediaries between individuals and the state as threats to true competitive, atomistic individualism. Mark Stallworthy (1989) wrote in the same place of 'Central Government and Local Government: the Uses and Abuses of Constitutional Hegemony.' It was an almost definitive listing of the extent to which the powers and discretion of local government have been radically diminished (contrary to Tory tradition quite as much as to Labour's). He sees it as a new, imposed constitutional settlement, and concludes: 'A constitutional settlement which is resistant to dialogue and which confers an unconditional legitimacy on imposed central solutions is antithetical to reasonable expectations within a purported liberal democracy.'

There has long been a centralist tradition in the Labour Party. Old Fabianism had one thing in common with Leninism: that the party should act for the good through control of the central state, and a belief that most intermediary institutions were irrational, reactionary or obstructive. But there was also always a pluralist tradition, more concerned to do good through people, in ordinary social groups and communities, than to do good to them from however heavenly a height. This centralist tradition was unhappily apparent in the half-hearted support, if not open opposition, given both by Government Ministers and by many Scottish Labour MPs to the Devolution Bills of 1978. Things done by a Government simply for political survival carry little conviction among ordinary people. Yet the fear was real among Labour activists, in Scotland as well as in England and Wales, that the welfare state would suffer if central power declined, or if coalitions resulted from some form of proportional representation. That was, of course, before Thatcher's massive demonstration of how much of social welfare, not merely in the personal social services and housing, depended on the strength of local government. So in the last ten years there has been an extraordinary conversion among Labour intellectuals and thinkers to constitutional reform. It is hard to think of any prominent intellectual or academic on the Left who now makes the old Footite defence of parliamentary sovereignty.

Some of the reasons for this change are obvious: constitutional traditionalists, of both Labour's Left and Right, have undergone an experience of suffering under inadequately controlled power; not unlike aversion therapy. But there has also been a movement away from mere pragmatism in the Labour Centre and Right; a recovery of thought by the thoughtless, a reanimation of values. Among those values are a positive sense of community. At the same time, though for quite different reasons, former hard or obscure Marxists, in searching for a basis for an humanistic and liberal approach, have been rediscovering pluralism. Philosophically, they now say with Harold Laski that 'all power is federal'; and empirically they say that while class divisions are still important, other social groupings are too. Therefore the old 'class analysis' is too simple to describe the complexity of modern or post-industrial society.

These two groups have, together with Liberals and Social Democrats, swelled the adherents of Charter 88's call for constitutional and electoral reform. Charter 88 arose in London, with no direct reference to Scottish conditions, but a remarkable cross-section of people have come together convinced that, because of a breakdown of traditional restraints on which civil liberties depended, a formal constitution is now needed. I am not the only repentant sinner in their ranks now more righteous than the righteous already. In other words, they have reached the same conclusion as Jim Ross in his 'Farewell to Devolution'. Deals which cannot be policed are not worth having. The Government's contempt for constitutional conventions is turning wide sections of opinion towards constitutional reform.

The actual Charter 88 statement says only of Scotland that 'Scotland is governed like a province from Whitehall' (well-meant but not wholly accurate, considering the size, location and Scottishness of the Scottish Office). One of the Charter's eleven demands is to 'Guarantee an equitable distribution of power between, local, regional and national government.' So do even they see Scotland as just a 'regional government'? This is far less than the *Claim of Right*. In fact some of the original sponsors read that demand more radically than the bare words might suggest. The first Chartist article in the press was deliberately titled *'A Claim of Right for Britain'*. Its author (Barnett 1988) said that 'along with the sustained and detailed *A Claim of Right for Scotland*, Charter 88 points towards a new kind of politics in Britain.' He quoted from Neal Ascherson's (1988) Mackintosh Memorial Lecture:

> It is not possible to build democratic socialism by using the institutions of the Ancient British State. Under that I include the present doctrine of sovereignty, Parliament, the electoral system, the civil service - the whole gaudy heritage. It is not possible, in the way that it is not possible to induce a vulture to give milk.

It is only fair and honest to point out that what has so unexpectedly happened is that (we) democratic socialist thinkers in Britain have now stolen, assumed or simply inherited clothes familiar to Liberals since 1886. The political mix of a more weighty anthology, which rehearsed all these arguments, made that clear: *1688-1988: Time for a New Constitution* (Holme and Elliott 1988).

## Conclusions

National movements, like political parties, can spend too much time arguing among themselves. English Charter supporters, let alone Mr. Hattersley, need to be convinced that Scotland's rights go beyond being graciously given the powers of a hypothetical English region and some limited protection in a reformed Upper House. The case for English and Welsh regional government may be good, and may rest more on democratic and on administrative theory than present signs of any popular support. But in Scotland there is massive popular support for Home Rule and substantial support for independence, simply because Scotland's case rests primarily on nationalism and a long national history. How can fellow English be so obtuse as not to recognise that Scotland, for all the interconnections and friendliness, is a nation? Or so condescending as to think that what Texans, Bavarians, Quebecois, Gujaratis and Tasmanians do, cannot be done by Scots - that is operate a federal system without imperilling the stability of the state? Why should a federal solution be deemed impossible because of the numbers of English? It depends what constitutional guarantees are given and how and by whom they are guaranteed. Every federal system emerges from a different circumstance. There is no general model.

What if the Government refuses (as is overwhelmingly likely) even to consider the report of the present Scottish Constitutional Convention, let alone to empower a referendum? And what would happen if, as is at least possible under the present electoral system, the Conservatives retain office after the next election, or if a Labour Prime Minister tried to avoid the commitment his party appears to have made to create a Scottish parliament? There is no knowing. Opinion might grow stronger but still not translate into appropriate, understandable, historically precedented behaviour. Or there could be widespread popular protest and real trouble. My vision of civil disobedience is neither of riots, nor of Jim Sillars and Donald Dewar politely disputing who shall cast the first symbolic stone at the windows of the Secretary of State for Scotland, but of respectable, worried, conventional local government officers all over Scotland beginning to ignore injunctions and to organise an election for a Scottish Parliament.

The heroic version of Irish independence centres on fighting, bloodshed, atrocities and 'the lads of the column', and the realistic version on the resulting stalemate and war-weariness on both sides. But there is a civilian version also: that at some stage law-abiding and home-abiding family men in three-piece suits and watch chains began to post their official returns on this and that to Leinster House and not the Castle.  Pray God Scotland's right can be obtained peaceably and without 'troubles'.  Much will depend  on the character of the response when propositions are made.  It will be a test for the English political mind at a bad time.  It is dangerous to affront the rights and pride of a nation for whom the present English Government has lost politically all right to speak.  The matter of Scotland, as Burke said of the matter of taxation, 'goes to the heart of the whole constitution'; and it finds it wanting.

## Notes

1.  Elie Kedourie (1960) famously argued that nationalism as a doctrine claims that for every nation there must be a state, but in that case national identity or cultural nationalism may sometimes, at least, stop short of being a 'doctrine'.  See Gellner 1983, Smith 1979 and Crick 1982.
2.  See especially Harden and Lewis (1986), Holme and Elliott (1988), especially Vernon Bogdanor's essay, 'Britain and Europe: the Myth of Sovereignty', also Bogdanor (1979) and Wright (1986).  To this should be added a virtual editorial campaign for reform in *The Independent, The Guardian, The New Statesman and Society* and *The Observer*; and also the activities of the thoughtful Centre for Constitutional Reform and of the campaigning Charter 88.
3.  See Pocock (1975: 603), his famous attack on Anglocentric history as being a misreading even of English history, in fact 'a plural history of a group of cultures...'
4.  The 'Church and Nation' report in Church of Scotland (1989: 144-52) contains an interesting account of the historical role of the Church in Scottish life and a claim that it has always opposed on theological grounds 'the alien English constitutional doctrine of the unlimited sovereignty of the British Parliament' (p.148).
5.  *Hansard's Parliamentary History,* XVI, p. 108.
6.  Ibid., p. 109

## References

Ascherson, N. (1988) 'Ancient Britains and the Republican Dream', in N. Ascherson, *Games with Shadows,* Radius.
Barker, E. (1945) *Essays on Government,* Oxford University Press.
Barnett, A. (1988) 'A Claim of Right for Britain', *New Statesman and Society,* 2 December, 14-15.
Bogdanor, V. (1979) *Devolution,* Oxford University Press.

Burke, E. (1908) *Speeches and Letters on American Affairs,* London, Everyman's Library, Dent.

Campaign for a Scottish Assembly (1988) *A Claim of Right for Scotland,* Edinburgh. Reprinted in O.D. Edwards (ed.) (1989) *A Claim of Right for Scotland,* Edinburgh University Press.

Church of Scotland (1989) *Reports to the General Assembly.*

Coupland, Sir R. (1954) 'The English Interlude' in Sir R. Coupland, *Welsh and Scottish Nationalism*, London, Collins.

Crick, B. (1982) 'A Defence of Politics against Nationalism' in B. Crick, *In Defence of Politics,* 2nd ed., London, Penguin.

Crick, B. (1986) 'Northern Ireland and the Concept of Consent' in C. Harlow (ed.) *Public Law and Politics,* London, Sweet and Maxwell

Crick, B. (1988) 'An Englishman Considers His Passport', *Irish Review.*

Crick, B. (1989) *Labour and Scotland's Right*, Tranent, East Lothian Labour Party.

Drucker, H. (ed.) (1982) *John P. Mackintosh on Scotland,* London, Longman.

Foster, R. (1988) *Modern Ireland,* London, Allen Lane.

Gellner, E. (1983) *Nations and Nationalism,* Oxford, Basil Blackwell.

Grant, W. (1989) 'The Erosion of Intermediary Institutions', *Political Quarterly,* 60, 10-21.

Hadden, T. and Boyle, K. (1989) *The Anglo Irish Agreement*: *Commentary, Text and Official Review*, London, Sweet and Maxwell.

Harden, I. and Lewis, N. (1986) *The Noble Lie*, London, Hutchinson.

Holme, R. and Elliot, M. (1988) 1688-1988: *Time for a New Constitution,* London, Macmillan.

Kedourie, E. (1960) *Nationalism*, London, Hutchinson.

Mackintosh, J.P. (1977) *The Case for a Scottish Parliament*, Tranent, East Lothian Labour Party.

Pocock, J.G.A. (1957) *The Ancient Constitution and the Feudal Law*, Cambridge University Press.

Pocock, J.G.A. (1972) 'Burke and the Ancient Constitution', in J.G.A. Pocock, *Politics, Language and Time*, London, Methuen.

Pocock, J.G.A. (1975) 'British History: A Plea for a New Subject', *Journal of Modern History*, 47, 601-21.

Prebble, J. (1988) *The King's Jaunt: George IV in Scotland, 1822,* London, Collins.

Ross, J. (1988) 'A Fond Farewell to Devolution', *Radical Scotland.*

Smith, A.D. (1979) *Nationalist Movements in the Twentieth Century,* Oxford University Press.

Stallworthy, M. (1989) 'Central Government and Local Government: The Uses and Abuses of Constitutional Hegemony', *Political Quarterly*, 60, 22-7.
Wright, A. (1986) 'The Politics of Constitutional Reform', *Political Quarterly*, 47, 414-25.